Running with Joy

LEADERSHIP AND LIFE LESSONS
MY DOG, BENTLEY, TAUGHT ME

Robb Hiller

TYNDALE
MOMENTUM®

The Tyndale nonfiction imprint

Visit Tyndale online at tyndale.com.

Visit Tyndale Momentum online at tyndalemomentum.com.

robbhiller.com

TYNDALE, Tyndale's quill logo, *Tyndale Momentum*, and the Tyndale Momentum logo are registered trademarks of Tyndale House Ministries. Tyndale Momentum is the nonfiction imprint of Tyndale House Publishers, Carol Stream, Illinois.

Running with Joy: Leadership and Life Lessons My Dog, Bentley, Taught Me

For information about special discounts for bulk purchases, please contact Tyndale House Publishers at csresponse@tyndale.com, or call 1-855-277-9400.

Library of Congress Cataloging-in-Publication Data
Names: Hiller, Robb, author.
Title: Running with joy : leadership and life lessons my dog, Bentley,
   taught me / Robb Hiller.
Description: Carol Stream : Tyndale House Publishers, 2021. | Includes
   bibliographical references.
Identifiers: LCCN 2021007060 (print) | LCCN 2021007061 (ebook) | ISBN
   9781496449696 (hardcover) | ISBN 9781496449702 (kindle edition) | ISBN
   9781496449719 (epub) | ISBN 9781496449726 (epub)
Subjects: LCSH: Success in business. | Creative ability in business. |
   Happiness.
Classification: LCC HF5386 .H6135 2021 (print) | LCC HF5386 (ebook) | DDC
   658.4/09--dc23
LC record available at https://lccn.loc.gov/2021007060
LC ebook record available at https://lccn.loc.gov/2021007061

Printed in the United States of America

27	26	25	24	23	22	21
7	6	5	4	3	2	1

Pam, without your incredible ability to watch over the details of the business and be a wife, mom, and friend, I would never be able to do what I am called to do. Love you!

Contents

INTRODUCTION *I*

CHAPTER 1: **The Joy of Knowing Who You Are** *5*
The first step toward becoming a true leader is to discover your hidden talents and find the real you.

CHAPTER 2: **The Joy of Being Who You Are** *27*
Talent is like raw material; you need to make something out of it through practice.

CHAPTER 3: **The Joy of Unleashing Your Talents** *51*
Life is full of change, and you are always learning.

CHAPTER 4: **The Joy of Shaking It Off and Picking Up Your Poop** *73*
To gain control of yourself, you need to acquire emotional intelligence, take personal responsibility, and learn the art of forgiveness.

CHAPTER 5: **The Joy of Guiding Others** *93*
Just as others have coached you, you need to learn to coach others.

CHAPTER 6: **Running with Joy** *115*
Success in life follows when you take on the attitude of a leader.

NOTES *129*

ACKNOWLEDGMENTS *133*

ABOUT THE AUTHOR *135*

Introduction

AFTER NEARLY EIGHT YEARS as the CEO of a high-tech company and twenty-five years as an executive consultant, I can honestly say that the biggest problem all businesses face is *people*. The day after I sold my company, I felt a huge load lift off my shoulders. I had been weighed down with people problems. Sure, I struggled with strategy and marketing and sales, but the most widespread challenge was people. Virtually every business leader I've met agrees.

But I've noticed something else. I've looked at successful businesses and wondered how they became so successful. It's the same answer: people! How can a company's biggest problem also be its biggest asset?

It took me years to figure out, but once I did, the solution seemed rather simple and obvious. *The difference between problem people and successful people is that successful people have tapped into their God-given talents and are in positions where their talents can flourish.* Unfortunately, only 35 percent of people are engaged at work,[1] which makes me conclude the remainder don't know their own talents—or, for some reason, they are unable to unleash them. What a waste!

1

Think what a difference it would make in total productivity if those 65 percent could be plugged into their natural talents. What if managers were able to select the right people and put them into appropriate positions to maximize their potential? They'd have a team full of self-motivated leaders.

What we have now, however, is the opposite. Not knowing one's own talent or that of others results in huge personal and business costs for everyone. The general symptom is that of being *stuck*. The sales department gets stuck, and growth suffers. Customer service reps aren't wired to be calm, helpful, and empathetic problem solvers, and a company's reputation is negatively impacted. New products are delayed and miss a window of opportunity because the team misses deadline after deadline. People feel stuck, and their morale seems to dry up and blow away. The company goes through burnout, lack of personal accountability, lower sales, and decreased profits. Everyone is dissatisfied.

Managers try to compensate by adding more heads, hoping to get unstuck, or they work harder to handle more tasks. Is that what's happening to you? Are you so busy in back-to-back meetings that you have forgotten or are ignoring your many natural-born talents? *People today are so busy with overloaded schedules that the inevitable hamster wheel just keeps going round and round.*

My solution? Don't be like that hamster. Try to be like my wonderful Lab, Bentley.

You've no doubt heard about Robert Fulghum's book *All I Really Need to Know I Learned in Kindergarten*. For me, it's more like *All I Need to Know about Leadership I Learned from My Dog, Bentley*. Don't laugh. It's true!

My British Labrador Retriever is a role model because he is perfectly in tune with his natural talents, and he is happy to be himself. He isn't full of existential angst or worry over whether he's doing the right thing. He is not misplaced, and he doesn't try to be something he is not. He is friendly and warm to everyone he meets, and every situation is brighter and happier when he is there. He simply runs with joy on instinct, and he has a good time doing it.

Are you tired of feeling stuck? Do you remember the passion, energy, and joy you had as a kid or early on in your career? Are you longing to rekindle that fresh excitement? Are you eager to run with joy, bringing that energy and hope into every situation?

Maybe it's time to take a look at where your talents are today. The greatness of YOU lies in discovering and using *your* God-given talents. When you know and learn how to activate this incredible set of riches—your talents—you will naturally head down a path of true meaning, and you'll realize better and more dynamic results. In fact, when you are in your "talent zone," you can do almost anything.

And, yes, I do mean anything! Which brings me to this question: *Which type of person in the world do you want to be?* There are two types: those who lead from their values and beliefs and those who are led by others. Which one are you now? Don't assume you have to be an executive or a manager at a company to be a leader. All self-directed people deserve to be called leaders if they believe they have much to offer the world, they know and actively express their talents, and they want to grow and make a significant difference through what they do every day. (I know of some executive assistants who are so skilled at their positions that the CEO would be lost without them. Conversely, the CEO could be gone for two weeks, and everything would run smoothly because the executive assistant is always on top of things.) In other words, *leadership is not a title but an attitude with a commitment to be personally accountable.*

I believe you can change if you open up and discover the greatness within you and within others on your team by following the lessons that Bentley has taught me over the years.

That is why I wrote *Running with Joy*.

If you're struggling to be effective in your role today, as I did for years as a CEO, this book is for you. In it, you will see the simplicity and beauty of what Bentley can teach you about leading. First, he'll help you rediscover your talents, and second, he'll show you how to help those on your team rediscover their talents by following the five-step process I have presented in the chapters you're about to read. We need to know who we are, be who we are, unleash our talents, shake off our worries, and learn the joy of being a guide dog for others. These important lessons will uncomplicate both your business and personal lives so that you can achieve greater success. You'll watch the clouds lift and the sun shine in when you and your people do what Bentley does every day—be who you are!

CHAPTER I

The Joy of Knowing Who You Are

*The first step toward becoming a
true leader is to discover your hidden
talents and find the real you.*

WHEN I SAY, "HELLO, BENTLEY," my British Labrador Retriever knows I'm talking to him. He opens his eyes, turns his head toward me, and smiles (as much as a dog can smile) to say, *I'm glad to see you!* Bentley is our one family member who will never have an identity crisis. He knows he is the kind of dog who really likes people and is always eager to meet new humans so he can share the love. He will run to you, looking up and wagging his tail, ready to cherish your attention. Bentley instinctively knows how to connect.

I was at the auto dealership the other day to have my car washed. With his usual smile, Bentley—without a leash—sauntered beside me into the lounge so we could wait together. A young woman who worked there saw him and flashed a smile of her own. She shouted from across the room, "Can I pet your beautiful dog? What's his name?"

"Sure," I replied. "You can pet Bentley."

She rushed over and started to pet him. It was just for a minute or two, but all the while, she couldn't stop smiling or talking to us. Once again, Bentley was working his magic.

An older lady waiting for her car chimed in, "What a beauty!"

"You mean me?" I quickly said.

She saw that I was kidding and laughed.

Thanks to Bentley, everyone there was happier than they had been. How does he do it? It's simple. He was born that way. You could say it's in his DNA, or it's his instinct, but I like to view it as his God-given gift or talent. Bentley was born to bring people pleasure and joy, and that's exactly what he loves to do. He doesn't try to be a guard dog. He doesn't even pretend to be one. He is a loving Lab whose goal is to make people happy by being who he is.

That trait was evident the first time we met.

When my wife, Pam, our son, Ryan, and I first went to pick out a British Lab, our hearts were open. Our old dog, Chamois, had recently died, and we really missed the joy and happiness that comes from a British Labrador. The way they greet you with a big smile (their tail wagging so fast you can feel the wind blow by you), you can't help but smile in return—regardless of what has happened that day. Labs love to play, too. If you throw any object out for them to retrieve, they love to run, pick it up, and bring it right back to you. Then the real fun begins. They sit beside you and ask, as only a Lab can, *Do you want to play some more?*

The breeder pointed out two puppies for us. She invited us to take both cuties over to an open meadow to let them show off. The black puppy ran off instantly. Ryan had limited success coaxing her over to play and cuddle because she was so full of energy. We could hardly touch her, and we could see she wanted to be independent. She was truly an adventurer. The yellow Lab, on the other hand, came to us to be petted. Then he started playfully flopping down on the grass next to Ryan, rolling over and over. How fun! And what an entertainer.

I had brought an old sock along. As I had done in a game I'd often played with Chamois, I threw it. The yellow Lab immediately fetched it, then ran back and dropped it at my feet. He was a true-born retriever all right, running everywhere with joy. Pam, Ryan, and I beamed. It was an easy decision, and that's how we came to adopt Bentley.

Even as a little puppy, he aimed to please. He was born with it. He's added immeasurable joy to our household, and he takes joy with him everywhere he goes. That's why I describe his way of life as "running with joy."

Why can't we all be like Bentley? Why can't we be happy just by expressing our natural-born talents? Why can't we make everyone smile just by entering the room? *The sad truth is that most people have lost touch with who they are or have never discovered their valuable gifts in the first place.* Such people seldom experience the joy of fulfilling their potential in a challenging environment; instead, they feel the frustration of trying to be somebody they are not. They even begin to doubt whether they can be truly successful at all. Others may have a sense of their talents, but they remain forever hidden in the wrong field or in the wrong position. It would be like locking Bentley in a kennel; he would no longer have the opportunity to share his gift of joy. If we want to be like Bentley, we need to start exploring our inner selves to discover our true gifts. That's step number one: Know who you are.

A Xerox Experience Not to Copy

After I graduated from St. Olaf College, a small liberal arts school in Northfield, Minnesota, I took a job in sales with the group insurance department of Washington National out of Evanston, Illinois, calling on school districts. What is ironic about this job choice is that my studies in college were focused on history, economics, and singing in the St. Olaf Choir. Hardly a recipe for selling group insurance! However, after one year of success, I had the opportunity to join the sales team at Xerox Corporation.

They recruited seven of us at the same time and spared no expense in flying us first-class to Leesburg, Virginia, for six weeks of training. They called our boot camp the Xeroid School. We were all excited because Xerox (along with IBM) was widely known to have the best training in the world for salespeople and leaders. (It became such a big deal that they started a division of Xerox focused on learning and development, which is still going today.) We learned all about xerography (a dry photocopying technique), products, speeds, paper types, applications, and—of course—we all enrolled in Sales 101.

After a few weeks of learning everything about the products and applications in our branch location, it was time for the big test. Our manager/professor assigned each of us a small geographic territory and told us to visit every business in person and "sell them a Xerox copier." Those were his exact words: *Sell them a Xerox copier.*

That particular advice didn't strike me as being quite right. That's not the way the Schwan's salesman did it when I was a kid. While I was growing up in a small town in southwestern Minnesota, the Schwan's man with his truck of frozen food would drive right up to our house and greet my mom. He always smiled and asked her what the kids were eating these days. (He was referring to my two brothers and me. Our poor mom was a saint—her ministry was cooking for three hungry boys and a husband.) That way, he found out where there might be a fit for his products. My mom always called him "our Schwan's man."

Needless to say, we ate a lot of Schwan's products and a

ton of ice cream. I was able to see that he, first of all, established a friendly relationship. Then he went on to serve our needs, instead of pushing a product that his manager had told him to sell. We didn't see him as a salesman but as part of our extended family. He was "*our* Schwan's man."

I recalled these memories as I knocked on doors all day.

At the end of our first day making cold calls on unsuspecting businesses, we all met back at the Xeroid School for debriefing. I had made twenty sales calls and found one business whose office manager was sick and tired of the office's old, smelly electrostatic paper. ·She ordered a small Xerox 660. No other students had any prospects or orders from going out and trying to "sell a Xerox copier."

My colleagues—and even our manager—should have seen how our Schwan's man had handled the process of finding out what our family needed and wanted. I was struck that one of the new sales recruits, Bernie, had made only five calls, and none had been successful. Although he gave many reasons for this lack of activity, the bottom line was that he really was not a salesperson. We confirmed that again later when we all took an hour-long aptitude test. Bernie and two others didn't score the minimum seventy-two points, so they were driven to the airport and put on the next flight back to Minneapolis. The four of us who passed were put on the fast track, but it sure didn't seem like a good percentage of success to me. And I was amazed that the others didn't study or take our training seriously. You could tell they really didn't like the role they were put into.

It is clear to me now that these three did not know themselves—and the company didn't know them either. The Xerox managers didn't take the time to dig in and assess people thoroughly, instead hiring based on college grades and whether or not they liked the person. If only they had followed their noses the way Bentley follows his! After a few sniffs, they would have learned that those three didn't have the right stuff to become salespeople. Bentley embodies what our Schwan's man knew: *The secret to sales—and business in general—is to build genuine human relationships. It isn't that hard if you are simply yourself and follow your instincts.*

But what if Bentley had been placed in the wrong job? What if he had been bought by a junkyard dealer in order to scare away intruders, thieves, and other dogs? I doubt that Bentley would have been successful. He would have welcomed people who weren't supposed to be there, let the thieves pet him, and played with the other canines. The junkyard dealer would have concluded that Bentley was a terrible dog—and probably would have taken him to an animal shelter. But I would disagree. Bentley is an excellent dog. He's just a lousy watchdog because that isn't his calling, and he doesn't have the right stuff for it.

All in all, my Xerox incident left me with two indelible lessons. First, my fellow recruit Bernie did not know himself. What made him think he could possibly be a salesman? It seemed obvious to me that he wasn't cut out for it. Second, why didn't our managers detect that earlier in the process? This could have easily been done by using more effective interview questions and a better assessment. The pain of regret would never have taken root—not to mention the expense of the first-class tickets, three weeks in Virginia, and six weeks back in the branch training.

Bernie was not a fluke, either. In conversations I've had with leaders, they agree that job satisfaction is often low. According to the results of a 2019 study conducted by the Lumina Foundation, the Bill & Melinda Gates Foundation, Omidyar Network, and Gallup, more than 50 percent of people are dissatisfied with their jobs.[1] Wow! It is obvious to me that many are unhappy because they are in the wrong jobs. No wonder we can personally feel stuck or we see people on our teams who are not excited about their jobs. That is sad and soul sapping! Their true talents can't shine in the junkyard.

Talent Defined

A talent is an inborn capacity that makes people highly successful in certain skilled activities. Some people are natural athletes, others are virtuosos at the piano, and yet others are born to sell. Tapping into your talent and expressing it through your actions is the recipe for self-fulfillment and a fruitful career. The key here is taking action. It reminds me of when the sales rep asks, "When will I get my raise?" And the boss quickly replies, "Your raise is effective when you are!"

If you don't identify your talents and exercise them, you won't develop your skills. The best athlete in the world had to practice many hours to go from good to great. Talent is not something you sit on; it atrophies if you don't use it.

Philosophers and religious leaders in the ancient world knew the importance of finding talents and developing potential. When Greeks sought wisdom, they went to the oracle at Delphi, where the inscription read, "Know Thyself." Socrates upped the ante and said, "The life which is unexamined is not worth living."[2] And in his teaching on ethics, Aristotle advised that the way to achieve *eudaimonia*—the state of human flourishing—is by performing one's "characteristic function,"[3] or what I call developing your inborn talent.

The importance of nurturing personal talent was even the topic for one of Jesus of Nazareth's famous parables. In the Bible, Jesus tells the story of a man going on a journey who entrusts his wealth to three of his servants. The distribution depends on their abilities, so one servant receives five bags of silver, another gets two, and the person with the least ability gets only one bag. When their master returns, the servants report what has transpired in his absence. The first two servants used the money and invested in various enterprises with good results. The first servant returned ten bags of silver, and the second returned four. The master praises these industrious servants and welcomes them to share his happiness.

The third servant feared for the safety of the money, so he buried his lone bag and returns it to his master intact but unused. The master scolds this servant for not realizing the value he possessed—and has him thrown out into the street to cry, forlorn, in the darkness.[4]

The beauty of any parable is that it can be understood at different levels. At the literal level, this is a story that praises investment. You must use money to make money. But this parable can also be understood at a metaphorical level. The value of the silver is the inner potential we have as human beings. That's the deeper lesson that Jesus was teaching. In other words, our talents are precious gifts, innate abilities, which we are meant to use. If we don't, we become lost in the darkness with no direction.

Plato used the same metaphor when he attempted to construct an ideal society in his multivolume work, *The Republic*. The key, he said, was to give every person a different role based on their natural talents. He explained that there are gold people (rulers), silver people (government officials), and brass people (laborers). A harmonious society emerges when they all do work that fits their natural talents.[5]

I think the same holds true in any organization. Your chances of success increase substantially if you have people with the right talents in the proper positions.

The Search for Your Talents

When was the last time you sat down and wrote out a list of your key talents, putting them out in front of you? We tend to take our talents for granted and forget about them, but we should, instead, take inventory of them often.

In Shakespeare's *Hamlet*, when Laertes is about to embark

on his journey to the university, Polonius, his father, gives him this advice:

To thine ownself be true,
And it must follow, as the night the day,
Thou canst not then be false to any man.[6]

If some of the greatest minds of Western civilization agreed on the importance of self-discovery and self-actualization, why aren't we better at finding and realizing our talents?

Said another way, why can't we be more like Bentley?

When Bentley was a puppy, we discovered early on how much he loved retrieving objects. I never had to teach him to chase after a bone, a ball, a shoe, a newspaper, or a Frisbee. He knew he was a retriever, and he was true to his genetic makeup. He was simply designed to retrieve with ease. The title of the Robert Redford baseball movie, *The Natural*, says it all. Can't we learn to return to our natural instincts?

After all, it's a travesty when people ignore their actual talents because they think they should do something else—something they aren't really gifted to do. How many people have you known who had a lot of innate talent that never seemed to blossom? While simple ignorance of their natural gifts can prevent some people from expressing them fully, others are in denial for various reasons. These are the really tough cases—people who have an inkling of their gifts but don't follow through. They often have a fear of failure, a lack of personal accountability, or a negative experience from the past holding them back.

Various factors can cause people to lock themselves in kennels, where they promptly feel trapped because they have forgotten that they have the keys to get themselves out. This book's job is, first, to remind you that you possess the key and, second, to show you how to unlock your kennel. Regardless of where you are in your career, it is never too late to learn to appreciate your God-given gifts.

Leadership Is Not a Title—It's an Attitude

Ideally, every employee at a company can become a leader and learn to be a positive influence in every situation they encounter. Such a business is bound to be successful. If, on the other hand, you are holding back on your talents or are locked into an ill-fitting position, you can feel inside that something is wrong. This friction between the real you and the false you sometimes results in a growl or a bark—or maybe just frequent whimpers. You are on someone else's leash, and it irritates you.

The most profound result of using your natural talents is that you become a leader. Your self-confidence motivates your actions, and you don't need to follow a script written by someone else for a part you were never intended to play. You are an actor, a playwright, and a director, free to create your own destiny. Otherwise, you are stuck and can only follow.

As Bentley would say, "Stop barking, and start leading."

The Rise and Fall of Jane

What about seasoned business executives who have been around the block? Do years of experience make that big of a difference in knowing oneself? In my twenty-five years of working with executives and managers, I would say mostly *no*. **Business people who have some level of success often get so busy that they stop growing and learning.** They are swallowed up in the daily grind of meetings, travel, and the pressure to get it done *now*! If they have a moment to stop and think, they ask themselves, *When will I get the time to reflect and learn how to be more effective?*

That's what happened to Jane, a charming and friendly director of marketing who was key to her company's growth for its first seven years. But then her department stalled, she no longer got results, and her people started missing deadlines. The grumbling grew loud enough that management reached out to her so she would get back on course. However, nothing worked.

When the CEO asked me to help, I met with Jane. Here was a successful, goal-driven woman who had somehow lost her moorings. I asked her a simple question: "Would you like to discover your greatness?"

Jane immediately said yes.

"Tell me why," I said.

She shared her story and told me all about her current job predicament. She believed deep down that she could do better, but she just felt stuck. It was obvious that her leadership skills had weakened because she was no longer self-directed in using her innate talents.

I asked her, point-blank, "Do you want to discover your greatness so you can become the leader and influencer you are meant to be?"

Jane couldn't wait to get started on a process of self-discovery. She took a full set of assessments that revealed her leadership style, motivating values, talents, and emotional intelligence. As we went over the results, Jane was surprised to learn that she had been unaware of both her strengths and her weaknesses. The more we talked, the more she could see that she had lost control of her situation because she hadn't been in touch with herself. But now she had taken the first step toward getting unstuck. She was getting to know the real Jane. For years to come, she flourished in her role and really made a difference in the company.

Jane's case is far from unique. Nine times out of ten, when a company finds projects are not getting done, it's because team members are not getting along. They don't function as a team because some key people simply are not good at what they do. Usually, these people were promoted, but they were dropped into slots where they didn't fit. You can solve two problems at once by pulling them from those slots and putting them in new ones that better fit their talents, giving them a much better chance to excel.

Your Behavioral Style

The good news is that even though many people have lost touch with their true talents, psychologists and social scientists have conducted a lot of research in human personality and our inborn skills. They have created various maps and charts in the form of tests and self-discovery assessments to explore the human psyche. It is a lot easier to embark on this life-changing journey if you have a map.

So let's begin your voyage of discovery and follow Bentley's idea of leading by better knowing who you are. I will ask you the same question I asked Jane: "Do you want to discover your greatness so you can become the leader and influencer you are meant to be?" If so, let's begin.

The following pages include a mini starter assessment that you can conduct yourself. Page 20 shows Bentley's responses, and page 21 has a blank assessment for you. This tests your behavioral inclinations and is far simpler than the full battery of assessments available for more intensive use.[*]

Step 1: Of the four words in each numbered row, circle the one that best describes you. Then count the number of circles in each column and write your totals at the bottom. Check which style has the highest total and take another look at the attributes of that style.

---

[*] If you want to take the full assessment and see fifty to eighty detailed pages about your values, acumen, and emotional intelligence, email Robb@performancesolutionsmn.com.

BEHAVIORAL STYLE EXERCISE (BENTLEY)

	GORILLA	HOUND	CAMEL	DEER
1.	DIRECT	(CHARMING)	PATIENT	ACCURATE
2.	DOMINATING	(OUTGOING)	EASYGOING	NO-NONSENSE
3.	DARING	PERSUASIVE	(LOYAL)*	FACT FINDER
4.	DEMANDING	(EMOTIONAL)	TEAM PLAYER	SYSTEMATIC
5.	ADVENTUROUS	(INFLUENTIAL)	COMPLACENT	CONSCIENTIOUS
6.	INQUISITIVE	SOCIABLE	(RELAXED)	HIGH STANDARDS
7.	(QUICK)	DRAMATIC	SLOW	OBJECTIVE
8.	RISK-TAKER	(SHOWCASING)	LOW RISK	EVALUATING
9.	BOTTOM LINE	(PEOPLE PERSON)	STEP-BY-STEP	ALL THE FACTS
10.	EGOCENTRIC	(ENTHUSIASTIC)	PASSIVE	PERFECTIONIST
11.	COMPETITIVE	(JOVIAL)	CONVENTIONAL	CONTROLLED
TOTAL:	**1**	**8**	**2**	**0**

BEHAVIORAL STYLE EXERCISE

	GORILLA	HOUND	CAMEL	DEER
1.	DIRECT	CHARMING	PATIENT	ACCURATE
2.	DOMINATING	OUTGOING	EASYGOING	NO-NONSENSE
3.	DARING	PERSUASIVE	LOYAL	FACT FINDER
4.	DEMANDING	EMOTIONAL	TEAM PLAYER	SYSTEMATIC
5.	ADVENTUROUS	INFLUENTIAL	COMPLACENT	CONSCIENTIOUS
6.	INQUISITIVE	SOCIABLE	RELAXED	HIGH STANDARDS
7.	QUICK	DRAMATIC	SLOW	OBJECTIVE
8.	RISK-TAKER	SHOWCASING	LOW RISK	EVALUATING
9.	BOTTOM LINE	PEOPLE PERSON	STEP-BY-STEP	ALL THE FACTS
10.	EGOCENTRIC	ENTHUSIASTIC	PASSIVE	PERFECTIONIST
11.	COMPETITIVE	JOVIAL	CONVENTIONAL	CONTROLLED
TOTAL:				

Step 2: Consider your behavioral style score. The highest number is your primary behavioral inclination, and the second highest is your secondary behavioral inclination. (Bentley's are Hound first and Camel second.) These descriptors give you guidance as to the primary talents of your style.

Step 3: Based on your primary style, ask yourself, *How can I use my talents more each and every day, both personally and professionally?* Write down some key ideas now.

1. _____

2. _____

3. _____

Your Mini-360

Eighteenth-century Scottish poet Robert Burns yearned for the ability to see himself as others saw him.[7] It can be unsettling to think that other people may know you better than you know yourself. At the same time, that's a remarkable resource for you. As you embark on your journey of transformation into a leader, get a little help from your friends, family, boss, coworkers—people who can be objective and sincere in their appraisals of you. A 360 analysis, as its name suggests, sets out to look at a situation from every angle. For your mini-360, you begin with at least two important perspectives: your subjective viewpoint and someone else's objective viewpoint. If you get more than one person to give an assessment of you, so much the better!

Change is scary for many people, and it is often more comfortable to stay cozy in bed like Bentley does sometimes—but those are times he misses the joy of finding the treats that are just outside the door. Once you overcome this fear, it is exciting to think you can make a change for the better. The same internal energy that drives your concern gets rechanneled to drive your passion for improvement. It's all a matter of attitude, and with the right mindset, it becomes easy to make the switch.

When I speak with executives about the need to find the hidden talents of their employees, many get the idea right away. Its truth is obvious, but they needed someone to point it out. That's all it takes for most of us. When you begin to know the real you, you get excited and refreshed. There is a lot to like about the real you, and it will feel good to get started.

Here's how you do it. Email the following questions to coworkers (with whom you have a good relationship) and at least one good friend. Preface the email with this short introduction as to why you are asking for their feedback.

Dear _____, I am reading a book called *Running with Joy* by Robb Hiller, and the first lesson is gaining a perspective of how people view my talents. Would you take a moment and respond back today? Thanks so much, as this will be of real value to me.

1. What do you feel are my strongest talents?

2. The book defines leadership this way: "Leadership is not a title—it's an attitude!" Do you see my actions as evidence of wanting to get better and having a strong desire to make a difference?

3. Do you feel I am personally accountable? Coachable? Any examples?

4. Do you have any suggestions that would encourage me in my development?

Thanks so much for sharing.

Knowing who you really are and becoming aware of your true talents are the first steps on your path. But, as I mentioned above, following up with action is essential. Raw talent doesn't mean a thing if you don't run after the ball to retrieve it. Having discovered your talents, it's time to manifest them by engaging in activities where they can flourish.

PAW PRINTS TO REMEMBER

❧ Knowing more of who you are is the key to finding your passion and purpose in life; self-knowledge can help you be more genuine and successful at whatever you're doing.

❧ When you actualize your natural talents, customers are more likely to appreciate you and want more of you. Do your customers affectionately refer to you as "theirs"? Do all the members of your team know their talents and feel the same way about yours?

❧ Don't let your soul be sapped. Knowing your talents will allow you to develop a vision. Increase your self-awareness by using scientific instruments, along with a process that includes assessments based on behavioral types. These tools will enable you to pursue the goal of getting the right talent in the right job. If you don't have the authority to hire, use scientific talent assessments to help you match your own passion and talent.

❧ Don't be like the servant in the parable who buried his bag of silver and became lost in the darkness! Know your talents so you can use them in the ways they are meant to be used.

CHAPTER 2

The Joy of Being Who You Are

Talent is like raw material; you need to
make something out of it through practice.

IT'S A DELIGHT TO WATCH Bentley's natural skills at work as he spreads joy to our family and the people he happens to meet. The gentle art of being Bentley, though, flourishes because his actions are rewarded and encouraged. For Bentley to manifest his natural love, he acts and reacts. That is an important lesson for us on our path to leadership. For our talents to grow, we need to be encouraged.

On a recent summer afternoon, our family dined on the outdoor deck of a restaurant. Bentley was with us, of course, sitting calmly by our side. After all, he's a part of the family! Some young children at a nearby table were intrigued by Bentley and started to approach him. One, a two-year-old boy, looked at Bentley, wanting to pet him. My wife, Pam, turned to the child and said, "You can pet Bentley. Go ahead."

The boy slowly put his hand out to do so, and Bentley gently lifted his head to be petted. The little boy shrieked briefly with surprise, but then his five-year-old sister rushed over and fearlessly gave Bentley a big hug. Bentley stood, wagging his tail like a fly swatter on overdrive, and the love fest began! A one-year-old, just learning to walk, joined his siblings, and Bentley immediately sensed that the boy was hesitant, so he lowered himself to the boy's level. (How considerate.)

All of a sudden, the five-year-old girl asked us, "Could we take Bentley for a walk around the deck?"

"Sure," we said.

Bentley joined them as they gleefully paraded around the deck. All the kids were giggling and having a ball following Bentley, our natural leader.

After the kids returned Bentley to us and went back to their table, their parents walked over and thanked us profusely. "Your dog really made our day!" they said. "Our kids couldn't be happier!"

I was proud of Bentley for another remarkable display of his natural talent. But then I thought, *Bentley is such a giving creature. What does he get out of it? What keeps him going?*

I soon realized that Bentley gets plenty of encouragement from the humans he interacts with. Each time he gets petted or hugged or praised, he receives a small reward that reinforces his behavior. He continues to act the way he does because it works. He gets plenty of loving attention (plus a nice home and regular meals). No wonder he keeps it up!

The same principle holds for other members of Bentley's species that go to obedience school to learn how to behave properly or perform tricks. Each time they display a behavior correctly, they get a reward, such as a doggie treat, a pat on the head, or a kind word of praise. Giving positive attention and encouragement really works to develop another's inborn talents.

This isn't true only of Bentley. Scientists define learning for all creatures as the interaction between instinct and environment. It isn't nature *versus* nurture; it's nature *and* nurture. This tells us two things right away: First, you have to act. Second, you have to act in a nourishing environment that allows your talents to grow to their full potential. Just as in real estate, it comes down to three things: location, location, location.

If two salespeople are thrown into the same territory, the one who does not have the right profile will falter, even if he or she tries hard, does all the right things, and is a nice person. But if you throw the right person into that sales territory, he or she will raise sales by 20 percent usually within 3 months. So, as you can see, it's a matter of talent properly matched to an environment, an interactive situation that becomes very practical indeed. It's about unleashing your innate ability to go forth and influence the outcomes of your interactions in environments suited to you. It feels so wonderful, yet it is also totally natural. Just ask Bentley—he will tell you that *the secret is simply being who you are.* When you unleash your inborn gifts, people will light up, and everyone will benefit from your success.

When a Gift Is Encouraged

When I was eight years old, my parents found a way to encourage one of my natural talents. I'm not sure if it was a random whim or if they did it on purpose, but it made a big difference in my life.

We were visiting my grandparents in Detroit Lakes, Minnesota, for the weekend. The relatives were sitting around the living room, talking casually, when my mother suddenly came up with an idea.

"Robby," she said, "would you like to earn some money so you can go down to the corner store and get some candy?"

Well, that was like asking Bentley if he wants to be petted. (Of course I did!)

My mom, who had always enjoyed hearing me sing in church, continued, "Why don't you grab Grandma's cup and sing one of the songs from Sunday school? Then let's see if any of your relatives want to make a donation."

I thought for a moment, and "Jesus Loves Me" came to mind. I sang the first verse in my finest soprano voice, aiming to please. When I finished, everyone clapped and then put money in the cup when I passed it around. Talk about instant gratification!

Now, I did not know if I had an actual musical gift at this point, but the strong response was more than just our relatives being nice. I apparently did have some talent, and this was the first time it was *activated* because people paid positive attention to me. I collected all the coins, put them in my pocket, and took off for the candy store a few blocks away. Wow, this was pure bliss! M&M's, Bit-O-Honey bites, and Snickers never tasted so good. I learned that people really did like hearing me sing, and they actually rewarded me with both praise and enough money to buy something I liked. These simple rewards—encouragement, recognition, and some candy, along with a sense of a job well done—set the stage and brought me confidence in my gift at that young age. It encouraged me to develop my singing for years to come.

When a Gift Is Developed

Years ago, I read an article in the *Minneapolis Star Tribune* that told the story of a young man, Ra'Shede Hageman, who became a star football player for the University of Minnesota Golden Gophers[1] and, later, the Atlanta Falcons. As a young boy, Ra'Shede had a strong sense of his athletic talents, but he lacked encouragement and stability in his life. Social services removed him from his mother due to her debilitating struggles with drug and alcohol addiction. The system sent Ra'Shede through a series of unwelcoming foster homes— twelve in all—so he only developed a sense of frustration, distrust, and bitterness. But he didn't lose the sense that he had a purpose in life. In a video he made for prospective adoptive parents, Ra'Shede said, "I want a family that will let me play football."

At last, his wish came true. A stable upper-middle-class couple adopted him, and they soon encouraged him to play football. Although his talents flourished in high school, he still faced challenges. He struggled with an identity crisis at times because he was African American and his adoptive parents were white, something his black friends didn't always understand. Yet when Ra'Shede graduated from high school, with twelve colleges vying to recruit him, he chose to stay close to home and his support network. He joined the Minnesota Gophers.

His hard work made him a team leader. His talent developed. Ra'Shede was rewarded with praise, recognition, and a college scholarship. Plus, as a star defensive tackle, he saw immediate results from his actions in the form of sacked quarterbacks and tackled ball carriers. As he moved closer to accomplishing his dream of becoming a professional player, he said, "Whatever team I end up playing with, they're going to get a hard, hungry, humble player."[2] This attitude—along with his talents, his dedication to his craft, his commitment to making a difference, and the encouragement of his coaches and adoptive parents—led to him being selected as a second-round draft pick for the Atlanta Falcons.

As Ra'Shede's football career progressed, however, he made some unwise decisions, which ultimately led to him leaving the Falcons and becoming a free agent. He has since acknowledged that these experiences humbled him.[3] This is a good reminder of something Ra'Shede said even before he was drafted: "Everybody has flaws, you have to understand. The fact that you can address your flaws and know what your flaws are, that's taking a step forward to changing them."[4]

Developing our "gift" can involve running down some roads that aren't the best. And we all sometimes achieve success but forget the foundations and lessons that took us there. Even Bentley is no different. I will throw a ball in the yard without letting him see where it went. Then I will use hand signals to point him in the right direction, and he will happily bring the ball back to me. Although Bentley caught on quickly to this at first, he sometimes forgets when months have gone by without us playing the game. Then it takes some more training to help him remember.

What I've discovered is that to run with joy, we must train ourselves to be humble, lifelong learners, or we will revert to old habits. But even when we do go wrong, we learn, we adjust, and we bring out the best version of ourselves. Mistakes help us as long as we are open to learning. When we discover this better path, we experience peace in a whole new way.

Practice Makes Perfect

After my debut as an eight-year-old soloist, I spent many years developing my gift for singing. In high school, I sang and played guitar in a special traveling group called "The Roaring 20s," and I also won a statewide music competition as a soloist. Such rewards prompted me to keep singing in college. That's one reason I selected St. Olaf College—I wanted to become part of the St. Olaf Choir, one of the premier *a cappella* choral groups in the world. It is famous both for the quality of the singing as well as for its vast and challenging repertoire.

With the encouragement of my professors, I worked hard until I earned a spot in this prestigious group. Membership in this elite choir was a reward in itself, but we were also rewarded with traveling and performing all across the country. We sang in places like the Dorothy Chandler Pavilion in Los Angeles, which hosted the Academy Awards more than twenty times, and at the Moscone Center in San Francisco. For our efforts, we received praise from audiences and critics alike.

This intense experience taught me two valuable lessons about developing talent.

First, *it takes a lot of hard work to make it look easy*. Learning to use your voice—or any other instrument—involves two stages. At first, you pay heavy attention to each specific thing, such as the notes of a new song, the strings on a guitar, or the keys on a keyboard. Then you repeat the activity so many times that it becomes a habit and you don't think about the specifics anymore. Once the notes become habitual and automatic, you can focus on the meaning of the music. You become an interpreter, and you are ready for the performance.

Our job as entertainers was to make the music sound natural and smooth, belying the many hours we put into practice. The football team began in August and was done by late November. The basketball team also worked together for four months. But the St. Olaf Choir was a year-round activity. We practiced five days a week for the entire school year.

The second lesson I learned was about *the magic of harmonious group activity*. Our individual talents melted into a spiritual oneness when we sang together perfectly. When everyone was in tune and we felt completely connected to each other, a special sensation emerged. It was an experience of synergy, where the totality was more than the sum of its parts. It was wonderful, and it produced beautiful music that the audiences *loved*. They didn't simply *like* us—they *loved* us.

Our choir literally harmonized together, but teams in sports and businesses also excel when they achieve a similar sense of spiritual oneness. Two football teams could be evenly matched in terms of individual talent, but if one of them achieves that perfect sense of harmonious collaboration, that team will run away with the game. It won't even be close. Spectators can feel that magic. They can almost see it. Everything seems to go right for the harmonious teams.

You can also feel this special harmony in businesses when all the workers collaborate with a seamless synergy. Their individual talents merge to form something bigger than all of them. Clients and customers can sense it, and they love it. It's the kind of magnetic pull that builds loyalty, and that needs to be encouraged in every team. If you visit a company, sit in on a team meeting, or walk through a factory, you can catch the spirit of what is going on. It's like running into Bentley on a summer afternoon: You can instantly feel the love. (And if it isn't there, you'll also feel it right away.)

This spiritual dimension of harmonious group activity is so strong that if anyone happens to be slightly out of tune, it's as nerve-racking as fingernails on a chalkboard. Your skin crawls, and it makes you shudder. Being *close* to the note doesn't count. In the choir, we were taught to help each other through such dissonance. If the person next to us was even a little flat or sharp, we would nudge her with an elbow or, during a concert, squeeze his hand discreetly. As members of the team, we were all responsible. We were all leaders. Any of us could break the harmony or restore it.

And, remember, *leaders are self-directed people who know their talent, commit to self-improvement, and take action. They not only want to make a difference in the world—they believe they can do it.* Within a team, the ideal scenario is when everyone plays their roles exceptionally and to the best of their talents. Everyone is singing the same song in tune and following the same conductor. That's when the magical unity lifts everything to a higher harmonic level. That is the magic of leading with love.

Vocation Versus Avocation

It is easy to believe that your unique set of talents is a perfect match for some vocation in life, a career in which you develop your innate gifts and earn a living at the same time. If your talent is fulfilling but does not serve as a source of income, it becomes a hobby or avocation for you. It may be intrinsically important as one of your gifts, but it doesn't offer that monetary reward that everyone needs. It is not always easy to make the distinction. In those cases, experience may be the best teacher.

That's what happened to me and my love of singing. After college, I followed the practical path in my career choice and became the CEO of a small high-tech company. After thirteen years, I had achieved real success, but I didn't feel fulfilled. I felt a deep yearning to sing again—and perhaps to find out once and for all if my talent was sufficiently strong to make a career out of it.

Then I heard about a music talent contest called the National Christian Artists Competition. This was similar to the talent shows on television today such as *The Voice*. I decided to enter the competition and flew out to Estes Park, Colorado, for the event. I failed to realize, however, that being over seven thousand feet above sea level definitely affects a singer's breathing capacity. Let's just say the air is rather thin and not as nutritious and filling as Minnesota air. I was gasping for breath the first day but managed to make it to the finals by the end of the third day. I was probably the oldest contestant, but I didn't care. I was there because I felt that the joy of singing in this environment would make me better, and I wanted to see where it would take me.

I finished fifth in my category and was thrilled to do so well. My performance attracted a talent scout from Benson Records, and we recorded an album in Nashville. (In those days, we actually made music on tapes and CDs!) I flew into Music City for my recording session with the Nashville Symphony as my backup. On the first day, I was so in awe of their talent that I forgot the words of the song. As I relaxed and started to sing, their flawless talent lifted me to a new level. When I heard the playback, I got tears in my eyes. Here was a virtual nobody singing with this group of pros, and the result was beautiful music. What a difference it made to work with that level of talent.

My recordings were played on radio stations across the country, and I was invited to sing on some television shows. In fact, one of my songs briefly reached the Top 20 on Christian music charts. But I soon learned that a good singing voice and passion for music are not enough to make a career. You also need good material. Otherwise, it's like a good actor who only appears in bad films. He needs a good script to make it big, and I needed good songs. Many novice singers bridge this gap by writing their own, a talent that I did not possess. I tried, but it was too painful even to think about. The alternative was to be famous so that good song-writers brought their songs to me. It was a catch-22. I needed good songs to become famous, but because I wasn't famous, I couldn't get good songs. I realized that singing was a gift I had to share, but it wasn't my calling. Singing was to be my avocation. And, thankfully, I discovered soon enough that my real gifts and purpose lie in helping others in business.

To find your vocation and your avocation, knowing your talents is the first step. Then get confirmation from your experiences and those who know you best—they can help you when you need to make a big career decision.

Professor Failure

This wasn't my first failure—nor, thankfully, was it my last. Failure has been a constant instructor to me, and it has given me wise feedback for next steps. Failure has allowed me to translate certain interests into hobbies and to walk away from others altogether. This is another talent I believe most people should foster—the ability to learn from our mistakes. Over the years, I have had many, many failures, and that has been a good thing!

Earlier in life, I fancied the idea of becoming a golf pro . . . until I ran into Professor Failure. I enjoy going out to play golf on a beautiful course surrounded by the smell of the freshly cut grass and the fellowship of other people for a four-hour escape. It is heavenly. The only problem is my talent. I am decent at golf, but to play at a professional level . . . help! Get me out of here!

This fact became obvious when I was seventeen and playing on my high school golf team. In one tournament, I had to win the eighth hole to continue playing. That hole had a river running through it and was a par 3 at around 160 yards. I stepped up to the tee and promptly choked, hitting the ball right into the river. That little splash was the sound of my golf career going underwater. At the same time, it was a wake-up splash, a lesson I needed to heed about my direction in life. Hint: This wasn't it!

That meant it was time to search for a new path, a new fence to climb, a new field to explore. Failure leads to a type of learning that only comes from experience—we can't learn it in a book. It leads to the deeper kind of understanding that King Solomon called wisdom,[5] the ability to make good decisions on the road of life. As we go on that journey, wisdom helps us find our purpose. It isn't easy, but wisdom makes it possible.

I knew there was a spark somewhere out there in the future—a flash of light that could ignite my talents. A little water trap wasn't going to stop me from finding my purpose and sending fireworks to explode in the sky someday. The same is true for you. Someday, you'll find your personal Fourth of July and light up your corner of the world with your God-given gifts—whatever they might be.

How You Can Genuinely Please Your Boss

You must keep searching until you find your buried talents and then let them loose to grow and develop. That's when you are on the right path as a contributing leader in every situation. Why, then, do some people insist on hiding their light under a basket[6] whenever they are around their boss? Your talents combined with those of your boss should be the recipe for natural synergy, but it only works if you are genuine. Whether out of fear or out of a misguided shyness, some employees can't be straightforward with their bosses, so they don't say what's really on their minds. They try to say only what they think the boss wants to hear, and they keep their valid but candid opinions to themselves.

Over the past twenty-five years, the top leaders of many

companies have told me they love people who are genuine, results-oriented, and straightforward. A president of one company recently said the one thing that really bugged him about his sales leader was his lack of honesty. The salesman is a great guy, but he is useless at truly serving his boss. The president said he lowers his expectations when he talks with this salesman and has to try to distinguish the truth from the other stuff.

Why don't we simply be who we are?

How Your Boss Can Genuinely Please You

Sometimes, it's the other way around. You may be perfectly prepared to be direct with your boss and share your talents with the company—but the boss is oblivious to your talents. How do you handle a difficult boss?

First, call Bentley to mind, and picture the happy tail wagging and warm smile he brings to all who call him to their side with a "Here, Bentley! Here, boy!" Now imagine taking him for a walk and soaking up the beauty of the outdoors together. After a short time, you will be smiling, laughing, and enjoying the image of being with someone who can bring out the best in you.

Bentley helps us improve our emotional intelligence, reminding us simply to be ourselves. He gives us time to calm down and let go of our frustration. The beauty is that we can achieve that same calm and peace by taking a moment and doing this in our thoughts.

What is your next step?

One of the main reasons people choose to leave companies is because they have a lousy boss. But there's another choice besides quitting—leading. How? Just as the singer who gets off-key needs a little elbow in the ribs, sometimes your boss needs a little reminder to get in tune with you. My advice is to take the initiative and sit down with your boss to have him or her participate in this discovery process you are going through. Make an appointment for at least a forty-five-minute meeting so you won't be rushed or interrupted. You may want to share the feedback you have received from doing your own mini-360 from chapter 1. Perhaps you can ask your boss to do the behavioral exercise and then compare your similarities and differences. This little effort will open up communication in a whole new way.

Second, share the simple exercise involving the six motivating values on pages 46–48. These are fundamental to your talents and what inspires your actions. Finally, list your strengths, and give your boss ideas on how to best make use of your talents. It's up to you! This is being 100 percent personally accountable. You can't change your boss, but you can be proactive and engage him or her in a wonderful discussion that may open up other ideas and opportunities that you two had never thought about. And remember Bentley's advice—just be you!

Beware of Ghosts

Sometimes, harmony in the workplace is corrupted by unhealthy habits, thoughts, or dysfunctions caused by past incidents that live deep inside of you. I saw this once while consulting for a software company. It was obvious that the founder, a technical guru named Mike, related to people in a totally different way from how Paul, the company president, interacted with them.

For one thing, they had different personalities. Mike was an introvert who had a difficult time communicating, meeting deadlines, and getting along with people. Paul was a friendly extrovert who communicated easily, met deadlines, and got along with others. On the second day of our off-site strategy planning session, I noticed that Mike was becoming agitated. It got so bad that by midday, he blew up over a comment one of the other leaders made, and he walked out in a huff. I called an hour recess and went outside with Paul and Mike to try to understand what was going on.

Both Paul and I listened to what Mike had to say. After a while, he calmed down. We returned and finished the meeting. I saw clearly that Mike functioned better one-on-one than in a group, where he somehow felt threatened. Instead of accepting or contemplating the consensus of ideas coming from the group, Mike reacted defensively. Whenever he sensed conflict, he lost all reason and reverted to a primitive jungle persona. He became like a tyrannical gorilla, pounding on his chest to assert his dominance.

Afterward, I met Mike outside again, and we were able to have an informal conversation. I wanted to find out why he felt so betrayed and why he hated the group telling him what to do. He finally shared the real reason. It turned out he'd had a painful and tormented childhood because his father had harshly criticized everything he did. Why wasn't he doing better in school? Why wasn't he better in sports? Why wasn't he doing everything that his father thought he should do? I felt his anguish as he told his story.

I finally asked if he wanted to continue to be kenneled up with these feelings of fear and rejection. He said no, so we took some time to review his full leadership profile. We focused on how he could activate his talents to strengthen his sense of self-control. Why should he still be haunted by his father when he could grow out of it by asserting his gifts?

I suggested he share his feelings with the team, and I explained why it was important to do so when he started to feel upset. It made sense to him, and he began to use simple words of self-expression to deal with various situations and people. I then encouraged him to ask for their thoughts. This worked better and better as he began to change his thoughts and communication style. It was amazing to see that, once he identified the hidden enemies of fear, doubt, and rejection, he was able to focus on being who he really was. He improved his behavior quite a bit—even though his ghosts and demons still visited him occasionally. But when they did, at least he could recognize what was going on and had a vocabulary and a thought process to deal with them. His efforts lowered the tension of the entire team and enabled real progress. Mike became happier—more like Bentley.

For Mike, the key was focusing on what he did really well

and letting it out in the open. The result was a much more fun and healthy environment! You can do the same when you reflect on what talents come to you naturally, asking yourself, *Is what I am doing today utilizing my talents?* If your answer is no, consider alternatives that would allow you to do what you do naturally. That could be a slight adjustment to the role you are in . . . or an entirely different role. But you will inevitably run with joy when you find yourself being a natural, just like Bentley!

Activate Your Gifts and Talents

1. To activate your gifts, look back at the two exercises in chapter 1, pages 19–24, and write down your discoveries in a simple list.

   a. My talents are:

   b. The common theme seems to be:

   c. Areas I might have thought about but have not focused on as my talents:

   d. Other:

2. Answer the following basic questions regarding your motivating values, and add the answers to your list. (See also the motivating values exercise that follows.)

   a. Where is my passion today?

   b. What talents do I most enjoy using?

   c. What types of roles or assignments are the most exciting for me?

   d. How would I describe my behavioral style? (See the exercise on page 21.)

   e. What motivates me?

   f. What talent or skill might I need to develop? Which ones are not activated as much as they could be?

   g. How can I be of help to others?

3. To gain feedback, share this information with at least two or three people you trust.

4. If you want a better relationship with your boss, share this information and the book with him or her.

5. Oh, yes, and if you really have courage, share a few of these types of coaching questions that your boss might ask to help engage a better conversation. Or, if you are a boss, consider asking each person these questions to build a company where inspiring "love" can be the difference between success and failure.

Your Motivating Values

There are six basic types of workplace motivators.

The following comes from research done by German philosopher and psychologist Eduard Spranger, which he described in his 1928 classic, *Types of Men*. This research became famous and is still used today in a detailed twenty-five-page assessment tool. Here are some basics to guide you in this important discovery of your motivating values. As you think through these descriptions, circle the two that best represent why you get up every day and do the things that give you intrinsic satisfaction.

- *Theoretical*: People with this motivator want answers, facts, data, truth, and knowledge for problem solving. They enjoy reading, researching, and solving problems with facts, data, and logic.
- *Utilitarian*: People with this motivator love the return on investment. They want everything to be useful and productive, and a financial reward is part of their drive. They view money both in a practical manner and as a way of keeping score.
- *Aesthetic*: People with this motivating value like things to be harmonious. They desire things to feel good, look good, and be pleasing overall. (This could be artistic, creative, or subjective in nature.)
- *Social*: People with a strong social motivator see potential in others. They love to help others live into their authentic selves. They love to solve people problems like poverty, homelessness, and other social justice issues.
- *Individualistic*: People with this motivating value like to be at the table when decisions are being made and

want to be seen as leaders whose voices are heard. They are connectors of people and want to be recognized if they do a good job. They are intensely strong goal-setters and want to drive change when needed.

- *Traditional*: People with this motivating value want to follow instructions and procedures. It is their system for living. They see the world in black-and-white terms and not too many shades of gray. They want things done correctly, with quality, and they believe in a higher power.[7]

My top two motivating values are:

1. _____

2. _____

Now ask yourself these simple questions, and then create conversations with your peers, team members, and boss:

1. How do my motivating values impact my actions and decisions on a daily basis?
2. Does my role or job allow these motivating values to be used and rewarded daily? If not, where could they be?
3. Are there additional projects that would tap into these motivating values? How can I make others and my boss aware of these opportunities?

PAW PRINTS TO REMEMBER

* People are key to helping you discover your God-given talents. Begin asking for feedback.

* When you stop barking and, instead, discover more of who you are, you will be in tune!

* With practice, you can be better together and activate everyone's collective gifts.

* Welcome failure as a teacher. It can be the guide you need.

* You will please your boss, your peers, and yourself when you are who you are.

* Focusing on your talents can overcome the enemies of fear, doubt, and rejection.

CHAPTER 3

The Joy of Unleashing Your Talents

*Life is full of change, and you
are always learning.*

BENTLEY AIMS TO PLEASE—that's what he lives for. But people sometimes get bored with the same old thing, so Bentley constantly comes up with new ways to bring people joy. He is always learning new tricks because he instinctively knows that *a true leader is constantly going forward*.

One day, I was playing fetch with Bentley, and as he brought back the rubber ball, he looked straight at me. He wanted to see if I was pleased. Maybe my smile wasn't big enough for him because, for some reason, he decided to do something novel: He spun around as if he were doing doggie ballet. I laughed loudly when I saw him, so he knew I was pleased. I liked it so much that I started encouraging him to keep doing it by calling out, "Go, Bentley, go!" It worked. The more I said it, the more Bentley danced.

Bentley now dances whenever I say this. When the kids come over, I say to him, "Go, Bentley, go," and as he starts spinning, the children burst out laughing, unable to contain their delight. They are mesmerized by this natural leader who never stops manifesting his limitless talent by learning new skills.

This dogged determination to keep learning new skills is a lesson for us on our paths to leadership. For our talents to grow, we need to be encouraged to unleash our gifts, which I mention in chapter 2. In this chapter, we'll look at ways to strengthen new skills so that we never stop going forward.

Such progress comes from retrieving, practicing, and developing our talents. This means we need to be coachable and accountable. I believe many leaders and executives fall when they forget what brought them to their current successful position. For too many, it has been a long time since they have thought about their natural strengths.

It's an especially good thing to remember your talents when you are stuck and need to start making progress. Don't let the wellspring of your success get buried in the past. Retrieve it and start doing something new with it to get you moving again.

Being Coachable and Trainable Will Take You There

One of Bentley's wonderful traits is his eagerness to improve with coaching from us. I grew tired of walking to the driveway every morning for the newspaper, so I decided to train Bentley to get it. It didn't take too long for him to catch on because snagging the paper is merely a variation on our game of fetch—it just involves grabbing a folded piece of daily journalism rather than a rubber ball. He repeated the action, I encouraged it, and it became one of Bentley's new skills. If I ask him to go out and get the paper now, he will run it back to me with tail-wagging joy. He knows he has found a new way to please me, and that makes him happy.

Are you coachable? Are you trainable? Are you willing and open to the idea of someone helping you move forward? Being coached can be the best way to break out of a rut. In fact, both words—*coach* and *train*—come from the world of transportation. A coach was originally a well-crafted wagon from the town of Kocs, Hungary. Then it became the name for various vehicles, from a stagecoach to a coach bus. College students in the nineteenth century started calling their instructors coaches because they were carrying them forward into new realms of knowledge.[1] So now a coach can refer to various types of instructors, but it still has that meaning of carrying you forward.

Train means much the same thing, and it originally meant *to draw*. People would say a locomotive is drawing a train of railway cars down the track. So to be trained is to have someone draw you forward on the road to progress by helping you develop your skills.

The next time you are stuck, find yourself a coach or a trainer to activate your inner talents and get you back on track.

A Leader Who Took a Page out of His Football Playbook: Greg Flack

One CEO who flourished by being coachable is Greg Flack, former CEO of Schwan's Company, a global multibillion-dollar company based in Marshall, Minnesota. Greg loved to play sports in college. He enjoyed the sense of teamwork, the intense competition, and the confidence of having a good coach lead the team. In sports like football, if players don't listen to the coach and play together as a team, they are no longer truly competitive. They can't win. Greg understood that and wanted to make a strong contribution to the team effort. He wanted to make a difference.

He carried those lessons with him when he went to work at Schwan's more than thirty years ago. His new coach was founder Marvin Schwan, who started out delivering ice cream goodies door-to-door, and he would also learn from the many successful assistant coaches who had grown the company for thirty-five years. Greg was pulled forward by Marvin's excellent coaching in two ways. First, Marvin kept promoting Greg to different manager positions of various divisions in production and marketing, until he eventually became CEO in 2008.

Second, Marvin taught Greg important values that were key ingredients in the Schwan's recipe for success. Like all business leaders, Marvin emphasized basic business principles, but he also made sure that all the employees were having fun and enjoying their work. You can't have a truly successful business unless the employees are enthusiastic and bring drive and a competitive spirit to what they do every day.

This human element is essential in relating well to customers, which brings up Marvin's great lesson about the company's purpose: sales. Its original name was Schwan's Sales Enterprises, Inc. That wasn't a very marketable name because people buy food, not sales, so they eventually changed it to The Schwan Food Company. But for many employees, the old name never stopped being the true meaning. Marvin always thought of Schwan's as a sales enterprise.

As Greg worked his way up the ladder in his early years with Schwan's, he found that one division he managed had stalled. Things weren't working, growth wasn't happening, and morale was low. He knew he was in a position to make a difference, but how could he handle a complex problem he had never faced before? The answer is that he *had* seen the problem before, not on the job but on the football field. He dipped into his well of experience and retrieved his old lesson about the importance of teamwork, and that was the answer. He took a page out of his old playbook and began to lay out a clear vision so that everyone would be on the same page, working together with the same game plan. It was essential that everyone be aligned to the same objectives, processes, and goals.

Greg reformulated the team by putting the right people with the right talents in the right positions. Don't we want that big guy on the offensive line to open up holes for the halfback? In addition, Greg made sure people acted like a team and communicated well with one another. Teamwork involves a lot of cooperation and mutual respect, and that means talking and listening. Once everyone is working well together and shares a clear vision, the synergy kicks in and they move forward. In this case, the division experienced a turnaround and, in one year, had one of its best sales years ever. Greg's solution used the strengths he had learned from his past successes and failures in competitive sports and beyond. He had become the division coach!

As a leader, Greg constantly retrieves the lessons that led him to the top. "I considered myself the 'Chief Talent Officer,'" said Greg, when discussing his approach. "I knew Schwan's could only get stronger by hiring talented people and helping those talents grow."

He also keeps close to heart Marvin's emphasis on sales. "I am all too happy to follow Marvin's great ideas and vision for the company," he told me, "because they still have the power to lead us to sustained growth in a competitive world." And Greg loves that competition!

Although Greg has moved on to other interests, he will undoubtedly continue to hold Marvin Schwan as his model, adding his own unique talents of influence and drive so that he and his employees grow together, have fun, and form productive relationships with one another. Oh, yes—and make sales!

A Leader Who Turned the Corner

Dave was the president of a small high-tech firm who found himself in the awkward position of inadvertently stalling his own company. Although he was a talented individual, he allowed some of his key talents to lay dormant, and this caused a blind spot in his management style. He was a techie, and part of his job involved making sure his workers carried out all the various technical projects that his company relied on—setting up computer networks, installing company-wide Wi-Fi systems, and so forth. He loved to measure the results and collect data.

The problem was that Dave forgot he was dealing with living human beings, not hard drives filled with data. He became almost exclusively task-oriented while giving short shrift to the softer skills, such as being nice and encouraging. But his obliviousness to this problem only made things worse, and it affected the entire company. Other executives became frustrated. Many of his direct reports were at a loss to know what to do, and the CEO wondered if he had hired the wrong guy.

The CEO expressed all of this to me one day in his office, and I suggested that if Dave were open to coaching and being held personally accountable, we could sit down and have an open conversation. We did, and it led to a live 360 review in which I worked with Dave directly and also picked the brains of seven of his colleagues to ascertain his basic set of talents. I knew Dave's leadership failure signaled that he wasn't using all of his natural gifts. He needed to have them coached out of him. The result was that Dave realized he had gotten away from many of the things he was good at, which undermined his leadership abilities and impacted the business negatively. His core problem? He needed to build better relationships with people.

After reviewing our learnings, I immediately gave Dave

specific steps to take that I knew would be helpful. For one thing, I got him out of his chair and away from his computer so he could walk around and talk with his colleagues. We are instinctively social animals, but that doesn't mean we socialize well if we don't get out there and practice. He had gotten offtrack with people.

Dave responded well and got back to unleashing his talents. He realized that he had been ignoring his great ability to empathize with people. Once he retrieved that gift and allowed someone to coach him on how to activate it, his work performance changed drastically—he walked around and talked to people, asked questions, listened more, showed empathy, and used his desire to grow as a model for others. Although he had forgotten what he knew, the coaching process allowed him to regain his talents, especially in the area of emotional intelligence. His team said he was more fun to be around because he had rediscovered the joy of practicing his many talents, and they were seeing better results. Not to mention, the CEO was much happier.

After another month of success, we focused on a key goal that Dave felt would make an even bigger impact in helping the sales team. We went through an exercise in which he listed his top five talents from the assessments, any areas that could derail him, and three vital behaviors he wanted to influence with the team. He also began looking at this talent worksheet on a weekly basis. In fact, I suggested a scoring system so he could know how he was doing. After all, he loved numbers! The result was that Dave went back to building on his talent and succeeding in his role.

Talent Versus Skill

Phil Mickelson is one of my favorite golfers because he is so incredibly gifted in using his wedges around the green. I know he is a huge talent in general, but his short game has made him famous and allowed him to become one of the world's top golfers. When I see his shots out of the sand trap, I marvel at how he can do it. As I've followed his lessons online, he's motivated and taught me to develop my knack for golf to become a pretty good short wedge player with my 60-degree wedge. When he has just a few feet to land a ball so it can roll up to the cup, he has the unique ability to take a full swing with a 64-degree wedge and land it right where he wants it.

Mickelson's ability is talent. His desire to practice this talent and hit all sorts of shots on a daily basis allows the talent to become exceptional. It goes from raw talent to polished skill. *Skills are developed when we practice our talents and become students of whatever we are working at.* Once we have natural talent, practice is what can make us a total "natural" and outstanding in that gifted area. If we have average talent, we can practice all day long and get only a marginal bump in success. It takes both talent and practice to reach excellence. In other words, *an exceptional skill is a talent we practice.* Are you practicing yours?

Bentley tops everyone when it comes to bringing excitement and love to lift someone's spirit, and his lessons on how to practice talent truly show people how to run with joy. It is remarkable to see people's reactions when they encounter him. They immediately see how well behaved he is and how he has only love to offer. (As you'll see more later, Bentley knows his limits when meeting someone.) Once they accept him and invite him over, he will often lift his paw to shake with them. Talent and some skill training bring energy to all.

Lessons in Accountability and Coachability

When I was ten years old, I loved going to the store to buy a toy truck or get some candy. I wanted to go much more often than my parents were willing to pay for.

One day, Dad finally came out and gave me the basic wisdom of free enterprise: "If you want to buy a fire truck so badly, go out and make some money."

On that hot summer day, Dad left for work, Mom left for a meeting, and my two brothers were out with their friends. Being home alone, I decided to follow my dad's advice and earn some cash. I knew my mom had been to the grocery store and had picked up many frozen cans of lemonade—a favorite in the Hiller household. I also knew that we lived near a golf course. My plan was to open a lemonade stand on the seventh hole and get rich. It was so hot outside, I was sure those thirsty golfers wouldn't mind paying a quarter for a glass of lemonade.

I made batch after batch of lemonade and filled all the pitchers we had. I loaded those pitchers onto my little red wagon, along with paper cups, ice cubes, and a little sign I made that said, "ICE-COLD LEMONADE 25¢." Then I wheeled my mobile lemonade stand across our two neighbors' lawns until I reached the seventh hole. I parked my wagon next to the green and displayed my sign.

It seemed like every golfer who walked by was delighted to see me, and most of them bought a cup. They were all so nice to me, and one even gave me a tip. (I had never heard of a tip, but I smiled and accepted it graciously!) I sold so much lemonade that I ran out and had to go home to make some more. What a hoot! I didn't stop until I'd sold all our frozen lemonade.

My parents arrived home around five o'clock, and my dad immediately went to the freezer to get some lemonade. Of course, there was none to be found, so he yelled over to my mom, "Dorothy, where the heck is all the lemonade? I'm thirsty."

She walked over and looked in the freezer with disbelief. All ten cans were gone.

I had been watching this interchange the whole time, cringing and trying to stay out of sight. My dad yelled, "Robby, what happened to all the lemonade?"

"You told me I needed to earn some money for my fire truck," I told him, "so I did just that this afternoon." I explained what I'd done. A big smile broke over Dad's face. My mom started laughing. I took this to be a good sign.

"Good going," Dad said. "Now we are going to learn about cost of goods sold so you can repay your mother!"

That's when I was introduced to the concept of business expenses and the meaning of accountability.

When I think back to this experience, it's evident that I liked business and was always looking for a way to make things better. I found some thirsty golfers who loved having an ice-cold lemonade. I found a need and provided a solution. This became a pattern as I grew up.

Through the years, my parents continued to teach me the importance of accountability, and it is a gift I carry with me today. They emphasized taking personal responsibility for my actions—whether good or bad—as well as for my inactions when I chose to do nothing. They gave me an opportunity to demonstrate accountability every time they gave me advice on what I should do. Was I going to heed their advice or not? They rubbed this in with their constant mantra: "Listen to what your mom and dad have to say." This is called coaching!

At the time, like all kids, I rebelled at what Mom and Dad wanted me to do. But the lesson did not fail. I learned that there are both positive and negative consequences to what I do. For example, as basic as this may sound, if I did not mow the lawn on the day we agreed to, I received only half pay. I quickly understood the value of keeping my word.

More important, I gradually became more coachable, and by the time I was working at Xerox, the lessons I'd learned at an early age truly helped me be a leader. If I chose to heed all the great training I received, I found my results got better and better.

Yes, I had sometimes been slow to accept coaching, but my experience at Xerox took care of that with a public form of accountability that everyone in the company could see. Hitting my sales numbers each month was up to me and no one else, and I couldn't stand being at the bottom of the sales rankings chart! As further incentive, if we didn't hit quota for three months in a row, we'd be kindly asked to leave the company. So I listened and took advantage of coaching at every opportunity. Coachability and being personally accountable changed my life.

Passion Is Worth Paying Attention To

When you were a kid, what was your passion or natural inclination? What did you love to do back when you had enough time to do anything you wanted? You may want to retrieve some of your lost talents from childhood. It could make a big difference in how you perform as a leader today.

The founder and CEO of Twitter, Jack Dorsey, is an introvert. As a youngster, he used to play with computers and write software programs for fun. Another hobby was listening to police chatter on the dispatch channel. He noticed they spoke in a code of sorts—shortened words, phrases, or initials that meant something to all the insiders. This gave him the idea of putting together short communication bursts now known across the world as "tweets." This was his way of connecting without having to be face-to-face, which he preferred because of his shyness and a speech impediment. His talents became unleashed. His introversion and his enjoyment of reading and thinking have made a profound impact on how we communicate today.

What talents could you retrieve, practice, and develop into skills to make the impact that you are destined to make?

A Leader Who Saved America: Josh Chamberlain

The ongoing task of every great leader is to go forward and innovate. We live in a world that is constantly changing, so if we don't keep up, we will be left behind. Bentley must know this, because he is an innovator. I once put some treats in a spot on the counter, thinking they'd be perfectly safe there. Not so. Bentley simply put his paws on the chair and thrust himself up to grab the bag. Another time, he took a sock of mine and hid it behind a couch. When I eventually found it, I turned the incident into a game of hide-and-seek. One of us will have Bentley sit and stay while the other hides somewhere in the house. Once we sound the whistle, Bentley runs around looking for the missing person. When the hider is found, everyone laughs. Bentley the innovator never misses finding us. He has a special talent—a keen nose that will figure out where we are, even if we closed the door! He will sit and make a commotion until we come out.

Businesses that don't innovate lose revenue when some other company that's really moving takes the lead. In war, getting stuck in the field can mean death—and sometimes the fate of the nation hangs in the balance.

During the Civil War, one talented leader at a single skirmish, in a single battle, may have altered the course of the entire war. His actions may have changed the path of the United States as the Land of the Free.

Colonel Josh Chamberlain was leading the 20th Maine Infantry on Little Round Top at the battle of Gettysburg, Pennsylvania. Confederate General Robert E. Lee had made his deepest incursion into Union territory, and his powerful offensive was on the verge of breaking the Union forces in two, whereby his next move would be to swing down to the east and capture Washington, DC.

The Confederates were gaining much ground during the first day of the battle, and Union forces were driven back to defensive positions. Lee figured the weakest point was the far-left flank of the Union defensive line, right at a hill called Little Round Top. So on the second day of the battle, he sent a strong force led by the 15th Alabama Infantry charging up the hill.

The soldiers from Maine on top of the hill fended off the Confederates six times, but then they ran out of ammunition.

Any trained military commander in his right mind would have realized that all hope was lost and the time had come to flee. But Colonel Chamberlain was not a military man. He had no idea about the proper military strategy. He was a professor, an academic who had taught himself Greek and Latin. He knew more about rhetoric than cannons.

He had joined the war to save the American way of life. Turning around and fleeing was not a possibility. In his mind, a good leader always pushes forward. He knew his men were out of bullets, but they still had their bayonets. Chamberlain's talent was logic. He retrieved the bookish common sense that had been trained into him, and he did the only logical thing: He ordered a bayonet charge, something that was extremely rare during the early era of modern warfare. His men were trained to obey, and they were trained to fight.

The brave soldiers from Maine charged down the hill with bayonets as their only weapons. The unorthodox attack threw the Confederates off guard. Then the far-left end of the bayonet charge swung over and up like a wheel, capturing what was left of the 15th Alabama Infantry and taking them prisoner. From that moment forward, the tide of the battle changed. Some historians credit Chamberlain with saving the battle and the United States itself. Thirty years later, he was awarded the Medal of Honor for his gallantry in action.

At a moment of desperation when the Union was stuck, Colonel Chamberlain put it back on track by relying on his inherent talent of clear thinking and his practical skill of applied logic.

Fortunately, you don't have to fight in a war to demonstrate the same creative leadership. By relying on your natural talents and learned skills, you can overcome whatever challenges you might face. Like Bentley, you can sniff out hidden treats and find innovative ways to solve problems. Keep moving forward and running with joy!

An Extraordinary Sales Leader: Ric Cote

A number of years ago, I met Ric Cote. After having great success at another company, Ric was eventually hired by the CEO, Mark Sieczkarek, to head up sales for a faltering medical device company, Conceptus Medical Inc. in Mountain View, California. As in so many cases where sales are not going up, Ric quickly discovered that the current sales force was comprised of people whose talents weren't a good fit for the product. They had been successful reps for cardiovascular or orthopedic medical devices—standard stuff in the medical-device world. The problem was that they didn't necessarily have the skills to sell *innovative* technology to a new target market of OB-GYNs, and Conceptus produced a revolutionary medical device for women's health care.

Ric saw that the company needed a revamp of talent if they wanted to have positive change. So he recruited great new sales reps who knew how to sell innovative products.

One of the most amazing talents Ric developed into a skill was his ability to conceptualize solutions to problems by envisioning and analyzing the big picture—what we call *theoretical problem solving*. He could quickly see an issue and conceptualize a number of different potential solutions. He would then talk through those solutions with a few other people at the company, and they would move forward with a plan.

Ric's other incredible talents were in the people category. He knew how to be sensitive toward others and display genuine empathy. He understood that everyone has different motivational needs. And his ability to engage in proactive thinking helped him be personally accountable. Ric was able to unleash his talents, and Mark had the foresight to encourage and recognize these talents. The two visionaries made change fun, and they developed a great work culture.

In the early stages of a company, you need an extraordinary sales leader who can see things others can't. This person needs to inspire, be highly empathetic when a sales team is plowing new ground, and have the ability to make things happen with creative solutions. Ric had all these abilities, and under his leadership, Conceptus grew from a small, struggling $6 million company to a successful business making roughly $141 million in annual revenue.

Ric's uncanny ability to connect with people and inspire them made him an exemplary leader. Part of what made him that way was also his commitment to being coachable and his desire to develop people. I would sit by his desk when I visited the corporate office and watch how he handled the sales leader who had an issue or the salesperson who was all excited about a success she had just experienced. He listened, encouraged them, and used his talents to solve any problems at hand. And why? All through my time working with Ric and the team, he constantly tried to improve himself. He was coachable and accountable to do what he said he would do. And he did. Thanks in large part to his leadership, in 2013, a large company, Bayer, paid more than $1 billion for the business, which at one time was headed for the graveyard.

Activate Your Gifts and Talents

1. To activate your gifts, look back at the two exercises in chapters 1 and 2 (see pages 19–24 and 45–48). Review the discoveries in the list you have already completed.

2. What are your two top motivating values from chapter 2?

3. Complete the following exercise, and focus on your top five to seven talents.**

Talent Exercise

Here are twenty-three talents that you can rate yourself on. Ten is the highest score, and one is the lowest. For example, here's a glimpse into what Bentley's exercise would look like:

TALENT	BENTLEY'S SELF-SCORING (1–10)	ROBB'S FEEDBACK
3. CONFLICT MANAGEMENT	10	10 (He has a way of defusing any situation with his love and communication skills, such as wagging his tail or putting his paw out for a shake.)
5. CUSTOMER FOCUS	10	10 (He always thinks of the person he's with as his total focus.)
8. DIPLOMACY AND TACT	10	10 (He is always gentle.)

** If you want more information on how to complete the talent exercise, email Robb@performancesolutionsmn.com.

Once you've graded yourself, choose your top five by circling them below, and ask someone else who knows you if they agree. Ask yourself how often you can focus on and find more ways to use these talents!

TALENT	YOUR SELF-SCORING (1–10)	OTHER'S FEEDBACK
1. ACCOUNTABILITY FOR OTHERS		
2. CONCEPTUAL THINKING		
3. CONFLICT MANAGEMENT		
4. CONTINUOUS LEARNING		
5. CUSTOMER FOCUS		
6. DECISION MAKING		
7. DEVELOPING OTHERS		
8. DIPLOMACY AND TACT		
9. EMPATHETIC OUTLOOK		
10. FLEXIBILITY		
11. GOAL ACHIEVEMENT		
12. INFLUENCING OTHERS		
13. INTERPERSONAL SKILLS		

14. LEADING OTHERS		
15. PERSONAL ACCOUNTABILITY		
16. OBJECTIVE LISTENING		
17. PLANNING AND ORGANIZATION		
18. PROBLEM SOLVING		
19. RESILIENCY		
20. RESULTS ORIENTATION		
21. SELF-MANAGEMENT		
22. SELF-STARTING ABILITY		
23. TEAMWORK		

PAW PRINTS TO REMEMBER

❀ Your talents allow you to make progress when you retrieve, practice, and develop each one.

❀ You are at your best when you are coachable and accountable in the process of developing your talents into exceptional skills.

❀ You can change and get better when you return to the basics of knowing your talents and start focusing on these strengths. Coaching will rapidly speed up your success. Bentley says, "Follow me—and run with joy!"

* "Traveling back to the past" to rediscover what your passions were as a kid can be a way to unleash your gifts to solve today's problems. Consider one talent that feels instinctive to you, write it down, and imagine using it in many more parts of your business and life. Where might that be? Now ask yourself what you can do to get even better in this area of talent, and take another step forward. Congrats for taking that next step!

* If Josh Chamberlain defeated a division using what was available to him—bayonets—you can overcome any obstacle in your way with your own personal natural resources—your talents!

CHAPTER 4

The Joy of Shaking It Off and Picking Up Your Poop

To gain control of yourself, you need to acquire emotional intelligence, take personal responsibility, and learn the art of forgiveness.

IT IS FUN TO WATCH BENTLEY run out of a lake dripping wet and then shake wildly till he is dry.

More than simply being amusing, though, his simple and instinctive behavior is a profound lesson for us in dealing with our problems. When things don't go Bentley's way, he demonstrates his temporary sadness by putting his head down and his ears back. Sometimes he will walk away. But soon after, Bentley turns around and goes back to looking at the bright side, perking up his ears and wagging his tail.

Bentley has supreme confidence in his talents and abilities, so when things don't go his way, he doesn't get all bent out of shape. He just shakes it off and continues on his merry way.

This happened the other day when our family visited our favorite upscale hamburger place, Gold Nugget. We headed toward the outdoor dining area so Bentley could join us. As we wound our way through all the tables, Bentley greeted the diners based on how they first reacted to him, showing that he knows how to make others comfortable. If someone is cautious, Bentley will keep his distance and smile, wagging his tail. If someone talks to him with an inviting voice, Bentley will meander over and, oftentimes, sit down. If a hand is extended, Bentley will often shake it—or just relish the pats on his head.

On this occasion, nearly everyone turned and smiled at our lovable Lab. It was almost comical. A table of men were laughing and having a good time, but as soon as we walked by, they stopped their conversation and got up to greet Bentley. These men were in the middle of telling stories, and I bet they would have kept on talking had their wives walked up to them! But not Bentley—they fell under his spell.

As I mentioned before, however, some people are immune to his charms. On occasion, we will cross paths with a person who is not fond of animals, and Bentley's smiles are returned with a scowl. We have to cut this unwanted greeting short and give a deep-voiced command for Bentley to back off. His immediate response is to put his head down and ears back since he knows he has crossed the line. But Bentley doesn't sulk for long. He bounces back almost instantly to his genuine, lovable self. If we encounter the person again, he is careful to avoid showing the same friendliness. Bentley does not hold a grudge. He simply shakes it off, forgives himself, accepts reality, and goes back to being himself.

Facing Obstacles with a Positive Attitude

We can learn a lot about becoming a successful leader from Bentley's flexible attitude. When things don't happen perfectly or we get thrown offtrack by occasional obstacles, we can lose our way, forget our larger purpose, and forsake happiness and success. When something unexpected happens that sidetracks our plans, we shouldn't whimper helplessly at our plight. Rather, we should deal with it, let go the best way we know how, and then get on with things as cheerfully and positively as we can, effectively shaking it off and returning to our core values and activities. A practical way to do this is by asking yourself specific questions because this can lead to solutions rather than victimhood. These can be questions such as, *What might I do to move ahead one step? How can I take this situation and learn from it? How can I continue to grow and move toward my passions and talents?*

There are two basic types of obstacles that can derail us from the path of success.

The first category contains things that are thrust upon us and we cannot control. We may be thrown off course by the economy, natural disasters, or disease. A car could hit us while we are waiting at a stop sign, or a new competitor could come out of nowhere and wreak havoc on our business. We wonder, *Why does this have to happen to me?*

The second category contains self-inflicted problems—those caused by our decisions, actions, or inactions. When things don't turn out well because we have made a mistake, we can veer off our path to success—and we can cause pain, heartache, and discomfort to others.

In both areas, we must learn to respond to these negative events in healthy ways. If we let the circumstances bring us down, we become immobilized and ineffective. But if we can be like Bentley and "shake things off," even while enduring unpleasantness, we become more effective leaders who keep moving forward!

I have had many of these life events fall upon me.

Fifteen years ago, I went for my yearly physical, and everything turned out great—except for the prostate screening. My numbers on the PSA test skyrocketed, and I was immediately sent to a urologist, who did a biopsy. The test results were not good, and they discovered I had the dreaded "Big C": cancer. The doctor recommended immediate surgery.

It seems as though almost everyone has been affected by cancer in some way, directly or indirectly. You either have had it or you know someone who has it and is going through radiation or chemotherapy. My mom lost her life to breast cancer after a courageous ten-year battle. I had seen the pain and suffering she had gone through, and I braced myself for the unknown.

I responded to this devastating news by gathering a support team that included good friends, my pastor, and my wife, Pam. Since I had worked in the medical device field, I picked the brains of former colleagues and clients who were in the know about what treatment options were available. I discovered a new procedure performed by a robot, using the da Vinci surgical system, that gave patients a much better chance of avoiding nerve damage during the operation because it could "see" everything ten times more clearly. After meeting with five different urologists, I found one in Minneapolis who was using the da Vinci surgical system— one of the few in Minnesota at that time. I would be his thirtieth patient using the technique.

I was tempted to wallow in self-pity and ask, "Why me?" but I did not want to go to that dark place because it zapped my energy. Instead, I thrived on hope and optimism rather than fear by taking action to find the best treatment options. And I was lifted up by the support and prayers of many people. Thankfully, the procedure was a success, and today I am cancer free.[1] Nowadays, the da Vinci surgical system is used routinely in various types of surgeries.

But what happens when, in the midst of adversity, remaining optimistic, cheerful, and hopeful isn't so easy to do? Can we learn to more effectively deal with adversity in positive ways? The answer is yes—by expanding our emotional intelligence (EQ). Emotional intelligence is a key area that impacts all of us, and the good news is that our EQ can be improved!

Emotional Intelligence

Leadership begins with becoming aware of your inner talents, but long-range success also requires being acquainted with your emotions. Western civilization has long praised the value of reason over feelings, and philosophers often refer to man as the "rational animal." But psychologists (and advertisers!) have known for years that people are really driven by their emotions. We crave positive emotions like joy, love, and excitement, and we try to avoid negative emotions such as fear, pain, and worry. Since emotions are so primal and instinctual, we have to become familiar with them to have any hope of mastering them. We also need to understand emotions when dealing with other people—especially employees and customers!

The ability to understand and deal with emotions—yours and those of others—is called your *emotional intelligence*. The term was first coined by psychologists John D. Mayer and Peter Salovey and then popularized by Daniel Goleman, who wrote a book by the same name. In contrast to your cognitive abilities—your so-called intelligence quotient, or IQ— researchers now emphasize your emotional intelligence with a corresponding label: "EQ." While your IQ is fairly stable throughout your life, your EQ can increase the more you work at it. Research suggests a high EQ increases productivity and is more correlated to success than a high IQ.[2] In his own research, Daniel Goleman concluded that the key differentiator between star performers and average performers is EQ.[3] You will make better decisions when you improve your EQ.

Therefore, it is important to understand yourself and others in terms of the emotions that inspire, motivate, and, at times, obstruct you and them. Empathy is an essential instrument in the tool kit of all executives.

Negative emotions have the power to linger inside you and sabotage your success. Guilt, fear, regret, and similar feelings can persist as a heavy burden that weighs down your talents. Perhaps you have had a conflict with a coworker, and your feelings of blame and revenge dominate your mind to the point where you no longer function effectively at work. Maybe you made a big mistake at work, and you can't get over it. A high EQ means you are able to recognize such garbage for what it is, then "shake it off" and get on with your work. Perhaps a more apt metaphor here is to scoop up your poop and throw it away.

Emotions are also contagious. Research shows that one low EQ person in a group who is letting his emotions negatively influence his decisions will bring down the entire group's EQ.[4] Such a person can undercut the morale of an entire office. When it comes to dysfunctional emotions, one bad apple can spoil the whole bunch. However, a good leader with a high EQ can spot that problem and take steps to restore a better attitude and create a safe and sane workplace. If you know of someone who seems to be negative most of the time, have a conversation with him or her about the impact this attitude is having on the team, and suggest reviewing the first three chapters of this book. When people don't know themselves, they most likely struggle with being who they are.

There are twelve elements to EQ:

- Emotional self-awareness
- Emotional self-control
- Adaptability
- Achievement orientation
- Positive outlook
- Empathy
- Organizational awareness
- Influence
- Coach and mentor
- Conflict management
- Teamwork
- Inspirational leadership.[5]

As a consultant, I am often amazed to see how a low score in one of these areas impacts a leader's performance. One of the most common elements for executives is low emotional self-awareness. When they complete our EQ assessment, and we review the results with them, the areas that need work stand out, as well as how they can improve with some fairly simple strategies. In most cases, leaders can improve in this area in a few weeks by being more aware of how they feel about their daily interactions with people and how other people might be feeling. It isn't that big of a leap to genuinely ask others how they feel about a potential solution or issue or how their job is going.

When you listen and have a positive, cheery attitude, you

can brighten up the whole workplace—and raise the EQ of an entire group. Perhaps this is why dogs like Bentley are allowed into many hospitals to visit the sick. They bring joy and energy to those feeling unwell. When someone with a dog walks into a hospital waiting room, I've been amazed to see people smile, point to the dog, and sometimes ask the owner if they can pet the animal. Bentley, for example, visited me after a surgery. Despite my physical pain, my spirits lifted when I saw him!

A Leader with a High EQ: Rhoda Olsen

If anybody understands the power of emotional intelligence, it's Rhoda Olsen, former CEO and current vice chair of the board for Great Clips, a highly successful Minneapolis-based franchisor of hair salons. During her time as CEO, she needed to empathize with thousands of franchisees—more than four thousand by 2017—to persuade them to align with the company's objectives. Great Clips does not operate corporate salons, so testing any new design or process needs to be a true collaboration because it works best when the franchisees willingly cooperate. Using a heavy hand promotes conflict. That's why Olsen placed a high priority on building relationships with franchisees, listening to their concerns, and always admitting mistakes without dwelling on who was to blame. At the same time, she tried to coach her corporate staff to adopt a similar empathetic attitude toward franchisees to prevent a needless rise in negative emotions. Olsen shared a story about how shaking off a major mistake and starting over allowed the company to introduce a new salon design:

> Many years ago, we decided we really needed a new salon design, so a group of corporate staff members and a few franchisees got together and came up with a bold new design to totally change the way the salons looked. We had not changed our look for fifteen or sixteen years, and in the meantime, our market had become much more competitive. The dynamic had changed.
>
> So we went through this process, and we got a little bit offtrack. The design they came up with was not consistent with our brand, and it was too expensive. The franchisees were up in arms, and we had to regroup. It was a fairly contentious situation because it was expensive and there was not a lot of support for it.
>
> Add to this the fact that new franchisees are very fearful. And people, when they are afraid, do not always behave well. They are afraid because they have invested their life savings or child's college fund. . . . They are used to being in control, and they have been successful in their prior businesses. They cannot quite "shake this off." You need to just be there and listen.
>
> Finally, I sat down with my VP in charge of the process, and I said, "We have backed everyone into

a corner. We are all in our defensive positions. We need to figure out how to go forward in a positive way. We just aren't where we need to be, so we are going to back up and start over."

And it is really funny—we used those words consistently from that point forward: "We are going to back up and start over." It didn't get defensive. It did not blame anyone. It was sort of like shaking it off. We just weren't where we needed to be, so we just backed up and started all over. We knew there had to be a salon design that everyone would be excited about, and it didn't make sense for us to go forward until everyone was on board.[6]

Rhoda's approach worked, gaining her admiration as one of the finest CEOs in the country. Great Clips was able to get a broad consensus from its franchisees for a new design that was affordable and that strengthened the brand, which was a contributing factor to the company's growth.

Scientifically Proven:
To Err Is Human. To Forgive Is Divine.

When modern science agrees with the ancient wisdom of the world's great religions, then you know you have a truth you can rely on. They agree that forgiveness is good for you. It just so happens that showing mercy and compassion as a response to injustice is one of the best ways to "shake things off" and get moving again on your path to leadership.

The opposite approach is to stubbornly hold a grudge until you can wield revenge. It is certainly natural to desire payback and to harbor resentment when you are wronged, but that scenario is one of the strongest emotional obstacles to the productive activity of manifesting your innate gifts and talents. Look at all of the obsessive feuds that take place in workplaces and between various groups around the nation and the world. The Hatfield and McCoy mindset is instinctual and pervasive—but it is also destructive for both sides.

In 1985, researchers at the University of Wisconsin at Madison set up experiments to determine whether forgiveness is actually good for our emotional health. They examined ancient religious texts to try to define the concept of forgiveness, looking at literature from Hebrew, Confucian, Buddhist, Christian, Muslim, and Hindu sources.[7] It turns out showing mercy doesn't mean condoning what was done—justice is still desired.[8] The difference is an emotional release in the injured party toward the person who committed the act—and a corresponding release of resentment. It's not excusing the unjust action but changing one's emotional response to it by distinguishing between the act and the person who committed it.

The researchers conducted randomized clinical trials using people who had been unjustly wronged in various ways—women who were emotionally abused, incest survivors, drug addicts in recovery, cardiac patients filled with anger, those hurt in the workplace, etc. The studies overwhelmingly showed that people who practiced forgiveness experienced remarkable improvement in their emotional health. They were better able to "shake things off" and get on with their lives. Even the incest victims exhibited positive results fourteen months after the study was over, and some escaped debilitating depression.[9]

Science has proven what many have known for centuries—granting forgiveness actually bolsters our emotional health and provides a way of healing when we are treated unjustly. This is great news for all of us who may be carrying this burden. The study then devised a pathway with twenty guideposts to help people who willingly choose to forgive. The Enright Forgiveness Process Model comes down to four phases following some preliminary questions: "Who hurt you? How deeply were you hurt? On what specific incident will you focus? What were the circumstances at the time? . . . What was said? How did you respond?"[10]

The first phase, "Uncovering Your Anger," asks the questions, "How have you avoided dealing with anger? Have you faced your anger? Are you afraid to expose your shame or guilt? Has your anger affected your health? Have you been obsessed about the injury or the offender? Do you compare your situation with that of the offender? Has the injury caused a permanent change in your life? Has the injury changed your worldview?"[11]

The second phase, "Deciding to Forgive," says, "Decide that what you have been doing hasn't worked. Be willing to begin the forgiveness process. Decide to forgive."

The third phase, "Working on Forgiveness," leads you

to "work toward understanding. Work toward compassion. Accept the pain. Give the offender a gift."

And the fourth and final phase, "Discovery and Release from Emotional Prison," guides you to "discover the meaning of suffering. Discover your need for forgiveness. Discover that you are not alone. Discover the purpose of your life. Discover the freedom of forgiveness."[12]

A Forgiven Leader Who Forgave Himself: Jay Coughlan

What happens when a top executive commits a tragic crime? In the case of Jay Coughlan, the power of forgiveness made all the difference in his ability to rebound and soar as a leader. Coughlan had been rising through the ranks of St. Paul–based Lawson Software for years and had found success as the vice president of its health-care division. But, one day, he made a terrible mistake.

During his adult years, he had become best friends with his father. The two of them went on a hunting trip and had too much to drink at a bar one evening. Jay attempted to drive home drunk, but he missed a turn. The car left the road and crashed. Jay awoke in a hospital severely injured. He entered a personal hell when he discovered that his father had died in the crash—and he was facing felony charges. He had killed his father, and now he was going to jail. What had he done? What would he do now?

That's when he discovered the power of receiving forgiveness from others. He learned that his wife forgave him, his mother forgave him, his friends forgave him, and his employer forgave him. While no one condoned his actions, they separated them from the person and showed him compassion.

But how could Jay ever forgive himself for his horrible deed? The breakthrough came when he took to heart the maxim that forgiveness is divine, and he came to the realization that even God forgave him. Just as in the third step of forgiveness listed above, Jay looked at himself with new eyes and began living with a new attitude. He learned to forgive himself.

Prior to my accident, I was a very aggressive and arrogant individual. I would have run you over very easily. And now there was a bigger calling; there was a bigger purpose. My realization of forgiveness gave me a sense of serving a larger purpose than myself. I did not know it at the time, but probably the biggest thing it did for me was humility. Now I have more of a servant's attitude.

There were a lot of reasons I could have given up when I was in jail. My religious experience and sense of forgiveness gave me patience and peace, and it allowed me to sleep. It allowed me to keep things in a proper perspective. And doing that, it allowed me to come in and live another day, another episode. Whereas if you get too hung up on worry, it freezes you. It ultimately leads you to depression. Thanks to forgiveness, I did not linger on that guilt trip. . . .

So where is your foundation to deal with this issue? If your foundation is only your work, you are really in trouble when it goes bad. Or if your whole identity is just in work, you are going to be in trouble when it goes bad. Or you are going to be inflated disproportionately if it goes well.

Friends, family, and faith became the offset to help me get through any kinds of issues. So for me it's that foundational question: *Where do you go when things go bad? Where do you go when things are good?* You remain humble.

I miss my dad to this day. The only person who is hurt when you're not giving forgiveness is yourself. I believe you can forgive but not forget. There are business people that I do not trust and I would not work with them again. I have forgiven them. I can still go have lunch with them; they are not bad people. It was just a circumstance we were in, but I do not forget. So in my dad's situation, I have been forgiven, but I do not forget.

But if you can have that inner peace, it allows you to go on confidently with energy, which you are going to need [to be an effective leader].

Because of the tremendous support Jay received, he was given a reduced sentence—one month in jail and five months under house arrest.[13] His dedication to his job and his humbler attitude prompted him to handle assignments and take on responsibilities far beyond his job title. Jay went on to become the CEO of another high-tech company, XRS; he delivered the commencement address at Crown College in 2016; and today, he is the chief executive and managing director of Coughlan Consulting, which coaches other CEOs. Oh yes, Jay, Bentley is so proud of you!

Shaking It Off

We are highly gifted but emotional creatures who need to maintain balance to move forward as leaders. We must be constantly aware of when disruptive emotions stifle our activities. It may be trivial bickering with a coworker or a profound personal tragedy that gives rise to obstructive emotions. No matter the cause, our best response is to face reality without undue worry or obsession—and get on with it. Shake it off!

Emotional intelligence can help us stay on our path, and it is essential when dealing with others. Learn to foresee situations as Rhoda Olsen did, to circumvent defensiveness in others. Building high-EQ relationships will help our businesses succeed. At the same time, we must keep a proper humble attitude toward our work, following the example of Jay Coughlan. It is easier to place our various situations in proper perspective when we see the bigger picture, and that can remove unneeded drama from the workplace. We must always keep in mind the healing power of forgiveness!

Everyone I know has experienced an argument with a spouse, boss, coworker, or good friend. We all worry about too much but become more effective when we do what Bentley does coming out of the water: Shake it off!

Activate Your Gifts and Talents

EQ is the most important part of leveraging (or de-leveraging) your talent! Of five key areas of EQ—self-awareness, self-regulation, motivation, empathy, and social skills[14]—which one(s) might be holding you back? Here are some questions to ask yourself that may be of help. Score yourself on a 1–10 scale, with 10 being the best score.

1. **Awareness.** How self-aware am I of my own moods, emotions, drives? How aware am I of the moods, emotions, and drives of others?

2. **Self-Regulation.** When something happens out of the blue that I really don't like, to what extent does that send me into a tailspin? Do I suspend judgment first or usually judge and then get the information? How long does it take for me to go from "red" to "clear"?

3. **Motivation.** To what extent do I work for reasons beyond money or status (extrinsic motivation)— that is, just for the passion of achieving something meaningful with persistence (intrinsic motivation)?

4. **Empathy.** How well do I really understand the emotional makeup of other people?

5. **Social Skills.** How good am I at developing and building strong relationships with others and at creating networks?

PAW PRINTS TO REMEMBER

🐾 Shake it off. Science and experience from others say this is a no-brainer, but you may have difficulty doing it. Try it out by forgiving yourself for something you have done and begin to unblock those areas that may be holding you back.

🐾 Email or call someone today with whom you have unfinished business and begin a conversation. Simple!

🐾 Pick up your poop! One of the highest forms of integrity is simply saying, "I am sorry." Who needs to hear this from you?

🐾 Forgiveness is a conscious decision. It does not mean forgetting, nor does it mean you have to become a person's best friend. But it does free you to unleash your talents and move on in a healthy and productive way.

🐾 Take personal responsibility, and experience forgiveness. It is your path to freedom.

CHAPTER 5

The Joy of Guiding Others

Just as others have coached you,
you need to learn to coach others.

THE NEXT BEST THING to having a home on beautiful Lake Minnetonka is keeping a boat there. One of our favorite ways to become totally refreshed is to take a one- or two-hour outing on the boat. A few years ago, we decided to rent a slip with a full cover for our boat so we wouldn't have the hassle of always taking the cover off and then putting it back on after finishing our cruises.

Last spring, I drove out to see the boat. Since Bentley loves going to the lake, I took him with me to the marina. After a long winter with much snow, we couldn't wait to smell the water and hear the waves. We pulled up to the long line of slips with canopies, and Bentley bolted out of the car.

He dashed over to the row of boats, immediately went to our boat slip, and waited for me.

I found it mind-boggling that Bentley remembered where we'd parked the boat last October! But whenever we go out together, he always knows the exact location where we left it and guides me back to it. He performs the same service when visitors come boating with us. We typically meet our guests at the marina, but one time our friends drove out with me. After I parked, I jumped out and began heading toward the marina office to drop something off, but I let our friends know that Bentley would take them to the boat. Their faces seemed to ask, *Yeah, really?*

In doing so, Bentley demonstrated another natural talent that all leaders need to emulate—how to guide people. That afternoon he jumped out of the car, went to the small bridge that leads to the dock, and ran down until he reached our boat slip. Then he sat and waited until our friends caught up to him. When I joined them, I noticed how they marveled at  Bentley. They said something like "Bentley, thank you for showing us where the boat is." They became believers in Bentley as a "guide dog." And I think it helped make the outing one they would not forget!

Leaders Must Be Guides

Learning to guide others is the flip side of being coachable.
You sometimes need help to tap into your talents and find the right position to perform your best. The same is true for your employees. They often need your help to shine, so you need to learn to be like Bentley. Your job is to guide people when they need it.

Guiding people is not the same as bossing them around. Guide dogs aren't just experts at keeping their humans safe and ignoring distractions—they also instill a sense of confidence and security, and they calm "depression, stress, and anxiety."[1] Think about it in terms of emotional intelligence. Do you want to fill people with fear, frustration, and resentment over always being told what to do? Or do you want to engage them willingly in the team effort, give them a sense of purpose they can believe in, and help them perform with confidence? To be a good guide, you need a high EQ.

Bryan F. Rishe is a sales executive who practices what Bentley does all the time—being a guide to all who want help. A few years ago, Bryan joined a Minneapolis-based medical device firm, Tactile Medical, that serves people with lymphedema, a swelling of the legs and other tissues due to a disorder in the lymphatic system. He inherited a sales department in disarray. The CEO at the time, Jerry Mattys, wisely understood that he needed a strong sales leader and, to his credit, knew that making sales was not his number-one gift. But Jerry was excellent in allowing the strengths of others to shine. Jerry introduced me to Bryan, and the transformation of the sales team began. I quickly saw that Bryan truly believed in how he could help the many patients who suffered from lymphedema, and he deeply cared for the people he inherited and hired. Bryan was one of the main cheerleaders who continually led the vision of helping patients. Others in the field just followed his example.

Another key value that Bryan held was the desire to put the right talent in the right job. One of the employees he inherited was Harry, who had been a good sales rep before his promotion to sales manager. But Harry did not fit the role of a guide dog who brings the best out of each person. To him, things needed to be done *his* way. He squashed the creativity and gifts of many of his reps without meaning to do so. Even after he was coached, Harry inevitably reverted to doing things his way. Sales and morale went down. People started to leave, and complaints flowed in. Harry just wasn't able to be a "guide dog" and lead others in an inspiring way. He was a great person but the wrong fit for that role. We solved the challenge for future hires in that position by using our benchmarking science and assessment of the "whole person," including motivating values and raw talent.

Another example of Bryan's skill in letting people be who they are is the case of Jackie, a top sales rep at Tactile who left but returned when the promises made by her new employer didn't materialize. A thorough assessment indicated she possessed the two key traits of being personally accountable and highly coachable to make a good sales manager. Bryan assigned her to turn the West sales region around, and she did exactly that, eventually becoming the area director. The results have been satisfying for everyone involved—especially the many patients who are now *walking* around a mall rather than remaining in a wheelchair. Bryan clearly understands what Bentley demonstrates on a daily basis. He knows how to inspire and be an effective guide for others!

Research Confirms the Need for Successful Guide Dogs

The sad fact is that most companies are not successful in keeping their employees engaged in their jobs. It's just the opposite. In 2013, Gallup CEO Jim Clifton expressed that, per Gallup's estimations, "managers from hell" are what drive employee disengagement, and "active disengagement costs the U.S. $450 billion to $550 billion per year."[2] Most recently, Gallup released that employee engagement was at 35 percent. Of those remaining, 52 percent were not engaged and 13 percent were actively disengaged. While this is a marked improvement from previous years, it's still a tremendous amount of disengagement when only the minority of workers are "highly involved in, enthusiastic about and committed to their work and workplace." Among the majority, workers who are not engaged "are psychologically unattached to their work and company and . . . put time, but not energy or passion, into their work," and they "will usually show up to work and contribute the minimum required. They're also on the lookout for better employment opportunities and will quickly leave their company for a slightly better offer." Those who are actively disengaged are "those who have miserable work experiences and spread their unhappiness to their colleagues."[3] I've found this reality saps the creativity of people and adds stress to nearly everyone. The attitude is summed up in the title of my colleague Terri Kabachnick's book, *I Quit, But Forgot to Tell You.*

You shouldn't have to work in an environment where people are merely present and not engaged. ***You can help be an agent of change.*** If you want to make a real difference in whatever you are doing, you must win the hearts and minds of your people. Disengagement is the ultimate emotional washout in the workplace. People just don't care.

Successful Guide Dog Tips

I have spent the last twenty-five years working with leaders and their teams to improve results, and it is so rewarding to see positive change come from following the four steps outlined in the previous chapters:

1. Know who you are.
2. Be who you are.
3. Unleash your talents.
4. Shake it off and pick up your poop.

This next step in being an effective guide is having others truly identify with the vision of what you are doing and bringing them along on the journey. You must care about *their* success along with the success of the business.

When you are focused on your own success, you won't be as successful, nor will you experience the joy of helping others. So here are a couple of general guide dog tips!

- Put the right talent in the right job the first time. (It is proven that profits rise when you do this and become a successful coach.)
- Truly care for other people and find out what motivates them.

A Leader Who Coaches: Mike Max

My favorite sports announcer is Mike Max, sports director for WCCO-TV since 2019. He is one of the most giving people you will meet—and one of the busiest. We sat down to talk late one night after his WCCO radio program, *Sports to the Max*. In all of his sports reports, Mike reveals a zeal to find out what makes people tick. He told me one of the greatest "guide dog" leaders he ever met was the former head coach of the Minnesota Vikings, Bud Grant.

> One indication that Bud Grant is a great leader is that the players respected him. Back when he was head coach, there was no sign that reserved his parking spot at Winter Park. Everyone knew it was Bud Grant's spot. He did not have to tell anybody he was the boss; everybody knew that.

At a speech recently, someone asked Bud whether he would be motivated by coaching modern-day athletes. He said, "Stop. It is not the players' job to motivate me. It is my job to figure out how to motivate the players. It is not the players' job to try to please me. It is my job to figure out what motivates them. And it always will be."

The opposite of that is "It's my way or the highway. I am going to put your square peg in a round hole and you better like it. And you have no say in it." This is not a partnership, and those guys are never going to play for you. The team leaders are going to rebel and that is going to filter down to the other players. So Bud said, "I have to win over the players; the players do not have to win over me."

If he is trying to win them over and they are trying to win him over, then you really have something. You have a partnership. But some coaches will overthink it or they try to make themselves the hero. That's why a new coach makes such a difference coming in to teams of equal talent.

Most of the time the new coaches are not necessarily great leaders. That is far more common than the other. Part of the reason is because the players are not going to blame themselves. So when things go wrong, the players blame the coaches, and the coaches blame the players. Every time. It is human nature. It is hardwired. You don't want to look into the mirror and admit your own faults—and you compound that when there is a coach that they cannot trust. Or who they think has ulterior motives.

And if the leaders of that team figure that out about that coach, it is over. If the players and the team did not trust that coach, it is over. Fire him now, because it is done.

I think this is where sports and business are the same. If you don't believe in your culture or your leadership, you're going to have all kinds of conversations around the coffee pot that are not productive.

When you walk into a room and know what motivates each person, isn't it easier to guide the conversations and get things done? It is about being outwardly focused and helping others move the ball forward. Maybe it is time to throw the ball out there, more like what we do with Bentley! Bentley always brings back the ball to us with his tail going back and forth, eager for the next challenge. I think you will find the same to be true when you do this for others!

A Leader Who Champions Being a Guide Dog: Paul Harmel

If you have a child who has had a school picture taken, it was most likely done by Lifetouch. When our son Ryan graduated from high school, my wife, Pam, displayed all the photos from Lifetouch, showing him from kindergarten up through his senior year. Do you remember yours? As one looks back at the changes, memories of each year certainly flood a parent's mind. But it is not just us parents. Ryan sat and laughed in disbelief as he looked at images of his own awkward stages. Our lives are a collection of memories, so there is nothing quite like a picture that captures a point in time.

This is the exact emotional connection that Lifetouch aimed for and ingrained in its corporate culture when Paul was CEO. He is full of warmth and has a passion for touching lives through professional photography. That is part of why he changed the name of the company from National School Studios to Lifetouch. When you first meet Paul, you would never guess that he used to be the comptroller of Lifetouch, once one of the world's largest employee-owned companies. He is one of the most engaging finance people you will ever meet! This people-oriented culture was the driving force behind the success of a company that once struggled to pay its bills.[4]

One of the ways I help employees to stay engaged is to serve as a mentor by asking people questions about how they feel about things. I think most people know in their emotions when there is a conflict with how they are spending their career. So I ask, "What are your guts telling you?"

If they ask me what they should do, I don't think I should be the judge. They need to come to their conclusion themselves of what is right for them or what is wrong for them. So I ask them some questions: "How do you feel when you say this? How do you feel when you think about that? How do you feel?" These questions lead back to their own thinking and feeling because most of the time people are confused. It is not just logic; it is emotions, and they have not sorted everything out. So I try to help them sort it out and add logic and practicality to it. They come back and say, "Yeah, I have these butterflies in my stomach" or something like that.

Of course, when you are in a managing situation, it is wrong to be too concerned about their feelings because you have to be brutally honest sometimes. One of the biggest mistakes that a lot of managers make is being too nice instead of being direct and honest. You are not doing that person any favors because how can they change and/or improve if they do not have the truth? "The truth will set you free." So, as a manager, you are really responsible to speak truth. Now you can do it the Attila-the-Hun way, or you can do it in a more humane way. It does not mean you have no empathy or compassion for somebody. I have great angst over it, but it is the right thing to do.

One way that I help guide younger employees is by telling them a story of an experience during my early days with the company.

Unbeknownst to me when I joined the company as a comptroller was that there was a power play going on as to who was going to take over. The competition was between the VP of sales and marketing and the CFO that I reported to. Just a few months after I started, the CFO came up to me as I was preparing the quarterly financial statements for an upcoming board meeting. The numbers were turning out a little better than we had originally thought, so he looked at it and was checking and checking. Finally, he said, "Well, I want you to book a half million dollars in commission expense."

I said, "Okay, for what? Why?"

He said, "I don't care. Call it an accrual bleeding. You know the VP of sales; he will spend it anyhow."

And I said, "Oh, really? Okay." And I thought, *What did I get myself into?*

The last thing I'm going to do is cook the books. I thought this job was a mistake, and I decided to leave. But I also had to spread truth, so I prepared two sets of financial statements: the one the CFO wanted with the crude bleeding and the real statements. I asked the auditor to come over and look at my work to make sure mine was right. I told him what was happening and that I was going to deliver two sets of financial statements to the owner of the company. I told him that I was resigning. And he said, "No, no, no. Don't you dare."

So he went and talked not only to the owner but to the VP of sales and marketing. The VP of sales and marketing said, "Don't let that guy leave."

So the auditor said to me, "The board meeting is on Tuesday. I want you to be gone that day."

So I said, "Okay. I will be gone, but I'm going to be gone."

And he said, "No, no. Nobody is going to accept your resignation at this point."

So I said, "Okay."

At the board meeting, my boss was let go.

The point of this story is you only have integrity once. If you give up your integrity, it is a slippery slope. The chances of getting it back are not very high. And so you only have it once. And that was my trial, whether I was going to keep it, have integrity, or whether I was going to go down a different path.

I have told that story to a fair number of young people, and they have said it has really affected their lives. So when coming to those kinds of crossroads and going, you only have integrity once.[5]

Paul is a real champion of being an inspiring guide along the journey of life because he really does care and wants the best for each person. He sees the talent and helps guide people to where they will excel.

A Leader Who Nourished His Employees: Dennis Doyle

Learning how to effectively coach people gave Dennis Doyle a proficient leadership style that made Colliers International Minneapolis-St. Paul, formerly Welsh Companies, a success. He cofounded Welsh in 1977 and served as CEO from 1987 to 2010.

Dennis is also the cofounder of MATTER, a privately funded, nonprofit organization established to fight poverty, hunger, and disease by using corporate surplus.

Dennis's high EQ allowed him to focus on growing the talents of his workers instead of giving them all the answers. He found the secret to nourishing employees: *Give them the freedom to make up their own minds.*

Leadership for me was a very natural thing because I played a lot of sports when I was a kid. I came from a family that really stressed hard work and when you get hurt, you "shake it off" and even rub some dirt on it. So working on the team I realized that you have to put yourself last, and you have to put your team up front. You must help them in every way that you can. Let the people who are working for you do their jobs and let them do it really well by developing a strong team culture and giving them the freedom to make decisions without fear of making mistakes.

I served as a mentor mainly by walking around the office twice a day talking with pretty much anybody who was available, from assistants on up. In this way I could get to know my team and get a feel for where the company was, what was going on, who was struggling, and who was doing well. When people wanted feedback, I never told them what to do. I emphasized their freedom to decide how to handle things. I told them, "You know who your client is. How would you handle it?" They usually gave back an answer ten times better than I could come up with anyway!

So my role was not that of an answer man. I was really just engaging our people in their business and letting them feel confident that they could make mistakes, and nobody is going to fire them. I encouraged them aggressively to do everything they personally could do to take care of their client. Their client was everything. They did not need to do a long list of things to make extra money for the company, they just needed to do one thing—make sure that their client was represented as well as he possibly could be. If they did that, then business success would follow naturally.

I noticed that the confidence of each team depended in part on the respect they had for their leaders. For example, we learned a lot about one of our brokerage department leaders on the golf course one day. Our brokers are a very fun group, very entrepreneurial, and they make a lot of money. They're the basis of how our company runs. They are also very competitive, even at a charity golf tournament. All the brokers were standing around as the new manager came through to tee off. He hit the ball really well, and it landed about twenty feet from the hole.

All of a sudden one of our top brokers shouted out, "Bet you can't make it in two!" The manager got to be about a foot away and then missed again. And you know what? He almost could not recover from it the rest of the round. It was not anything to do with his skill; for he was a talented golfer. It had to do with the lack of confidence from his peers and the fear he had.

Team culture is like that. You really need to be able to put the ball in the hole when it's your turn. You need to step up at certain times; you need somebody who has your back, particularly the leader of the organization. Leading an organization takes a coaching style of leadership. It is not so much how smart you are or anything else. It is a lot more that you care about people and can your team put it in the hole at the right time? Can people trust you? People need to know that they make their decisions not based on fear but from the freedom their leader has given them to fail and the confidence that they are vital members of the team.

If you work at instilling confidence in people because they believe in the culture you walk every day, they will exceed your expectations. In most cases, they will guide you to where you need to be. And the times when things don't turn out the best, you can respond with confidence to new solutions rather than with fear.

Parlez-vous Français, Bentley?

Bentley doesn't understand language.

Or does he?

Some of the best times we have with Bentley are when he tries to communicate with us. He actually guides us so well—it's inspiring. When he was a puppy, I noticed that he listened intently to whatever we were saying. It was as though he was taking a crash course in English and figuring out how to communicate what he wanted.

One day, I yelled upstairs to Pam that the car was running, and it was time to go somewhere. Bentley immediately got up from his bed, walked over, and stood by the door to the garage. Needless to say, although we hadn't planned to do so, we brought him along.

The next time, we spelled it out—"C-A-R"—and Bentley stayed put. But then he saw us go to the door and leave. Days later, we did the same thing, spelling out the word, but this time Bentley actually got up and went to the door. Yes, we brought him along just because we admired his learning and communication skills. Our Bentley was learning how to spell!

Our final triumph came before another car ride. We fooled Bentley by speaking in French to each other, and that took care of it. Bentley didn't get up! But the *next* time we tried it, he again got up and waited by the door for us. Was Bentley becoming bilingual?

We realized that Bentley had not taken an online Berlitz course. He was simply learning to watch our body language as we were preparing to go somewhere. He was cuing in to our nonverbal communication. It doesn't seem to matter what language we use. He observes our nonverbal behavior when we're getting ready to leave and goes to the door because he wants to come along.

At the same time, he is an expert in teaching us *his* nonverbal cues. After we eat dinner every night, he comes by one of us and nudges us with his nose, getting fidgety. We ask him what he wants. He goes to the freezer door and waits. This clearly communicates to us that he wants a "dog frosty." If we don't respond, he comes back and asks with that *Please, Dad* look in his eyes. He continues with his nonverbal communication until it gets him what he wants. He has learned the art of successful communication without one word.

Nonverbal Communication

That brings us to a key element of being a guide dog and coach to the people you are with every day. We might assume that our main means of communication are through the words we speak and write, but that is not true. We communicate mostly with our hearts, showing it through our tone of voice, a warm smile, a touch to the shoulder, a look that makes one laugh, an open posture, and how we look at the person talking to us.

Since nonverbal communication is so important, you need to be aware of the signals your behavior and body language send everyone. If you control your nonverbal communication, you can use this tacit motivational tool to help coach others. On the flip side, if you don't pay attention to your nonverbal communication, you might be inadvertently contributing to the alienation of your staff. What impact might this have on the 65 percent of people who are disengaged from making a difference at your company or team?

I once led a strategy planning session for a company, and whenever a team member expressed an opinion the senior leader did not like, the leader crossed his arms against his chest and scowled. When another person piped in and liked the idea, the senior leader would get up and walk away for a short time, putting his hands on his hips and tightening his mouth, with blood sometimes rushing to his face.

Fortunately, our fifteen-minute coffee break arrived, and I asked the senior leader if we could talk briefly outside. I simply described what I was seeing and asked him how he would feel if his boss were doing the same things. He quickly apologized. He'd had no idea that his nonverbal communication came across so strongly. I suggested he make an effort to listen, take notes, and—when it was his turn to talk—share what he was hearing from the group.

Taking notes saved the day. It got him to listen rather than judge. He was able to reflect on what he was hearing. In this way, the best suggestions percolated up, and the meeting ended with clarity and clear action steps that everyone bought into.

The solution is simple. Why not try Bentley's more positive form of communication and watch how fun it is to be at work with engaged people?

Activate Your Gifts and Talents

Being a guide to others is one of the great callings for anyone who wants to make a difference. Remember, leadership is not a title—it's an attitude. Ponder the questions below as you prepare to read chapter 6, where I share my insights on how everything comes together so you can find yourself running with joy!

1. How well am I doing at bringing other people along for the journey so they will look back ten years from now and say, "[Your name] really influenced my life in a positive way and led me down the right path. [Your name] made a lasting and positive difference"?

2. Whom do I need to email or call to thank for being a wonderful "guide dog" to me? (Your action will be a pleasant reward for them, and it will make their day!)

3. What can I do today to help others become truly engaged and be more of who they can become?

4. Will I take action to discover what talent is needed in a role and put the right talent in the right job? (It is fundamental to everyone's success.)

PAW PRINTS TO REMEMBER

According to the most recent Gallup research, 65 percent of the workforce is partially or entirely disengaged—and that is shocking![6] You can be an agent of change by being like Bentley and becoming an inspiring guide dog.

* Learning to guide others is the flip side of being coachable. You can help bring others along and make a difference regardless of your title. It really is an attitude!

* Performance immediately increases when you match a person's talent (a person's behavioral style, motivating values, and raw talent) with what the job requires for superior performance.

* Your job as a guide and coach is to find out what motivates the person—and then do the things that bring out the best in him or her.

* Instilling confidence in people is one of the great attributes of a guide.

* Communicating your vision and culture with passion is key to leading, and it involves both verbal and nonverbal areas.

CHAPTER 6

Running with Joy

*Success in life follows when you take
on the attitude of a leader.*

BENTLEY IS A NATURAL-BORN RETRIEVER. When we throw a ball for him, he loves to run, pick it up, and bring it right back to us. He retrieves the ball with pure joy and full conviction because he is simply being himself.

Bentley shows the same enthusiasm when Pam or I call him to "Come!" He never simply walks over to meet us. He runs toward us as fast as he can, full of joy, because he knows we will greet him with love and encouragement. It is like going on a trip and returning home to see your mom and dad, kids, or spouse. The reunion at the airport is full of many hugs, big smiles, and true happiness. Bentley has that same high-energy drive to connect with people. There is nothing quite like the unconditional acceptance we receive from those we love and care for.

This intrinsic joy and self-assurance are what life and work can be like for all of us when we follow Bentley's lessons for success. Learning and applying these truths will really help us and our teams. Let's review Bentley's five leadership lessons:

1. Know who you are.
2. Be who you are.
3. Unleash your talents.
4. Shake it off and pick up your poop.
5. Guide others.

A Leader Who Does What Bentley Does: Doug Kohrs

One outstanding business leader who exemplifies Bentley's leadership lessons is Doug Kohrs, former CEO of two highly successful medical device companies, Tornier Medical and American Medical Systems, and current president and CEO of Responsive Arthroscopy, a sports-focused medical device company in Minneapolis. Doug is a true believer in learning who you are and then being who you are.

Early in Doug's career, he worked as a budding project engineer in Boston for the medical division of Johnson & Johnson. His team was having great success with their initial product, so J & J saw Doug's potential. They wanted to expand his leadership and develop his skills, so they told him to hire an engineer. Doug was only twenty-six, and this would be his first hire. He looked for the right talent and interviewed Jude, a young engineer from MIT, one of the best engineering schools in the world. Jude was just twenty-two, but Doug thought that he had great potential, so he hired him. Jude and Doug thus began a highly successful relationship and came up with many other innovative and-successful ideas.

At the time this was all new to Doug. He didn't realize he could be a leader without anyone working for him. He just wanted to make a difference. Doug viewed Jude as a colleague, not a subordinate. The two of them simply focused on the goal at hand and enjoyed working together to get the job done. In fact, other people in the company did not necessarily know who the boss was because Doug and Jude were so focused on having fun with their many successful projects.

Let's fast-forward to today, thirty-eight years later. After selling an orthopedic knee company that he started to Medtronic, he has started a new sports medicine company called Responsive Anthroscopy. He is also dedicated to helping a nonprofit that focuses on feeding the poor. When Doug has a problem to think over, guess who he calls? You guessed it. He and Jude are back working on various projects together.

"I am treating Jude the same as I did thirty years ago at J & J—as colleagues," said Doug.

Just like Bentley, Doug and Jude each know their own talents and come together by "being who they are," with no thought as to who is the boss, but rather focusing on how they can change the world together.

What is amazing is that Doug repeated the same hiring process at another med-tech company, but this time the prospective engineer had no formal education, just street talent as a mechanical engineer. Doug saw his work, witnessed his can-do attitude, and hired him. The two of them worked together for years to improve patients' lives. Doug pointed out that one successful engineer came from a top university and the other came with no formal education, just natural ability. The common denominators were talent and the passion to make a difference. It all comes back to the fundamental belief that *leadership is not a title—it's an attitude.*

When I asked Doug what lessons he felt others could benefit from, he said, "Do what Bentley does! Learning and leadership are indispensable to success. One of the great lessons I gained at an early age was the discipline of asking myself, *What did I learn this week?*

In other words, *a good week does not necessarily mean that everything went smoothly—it shows how well one reacted to the various challenges.*

"Many times, we learned the most when bad things happened, and then we figured out how we could best respond. This allowed us to gain understanding and get to the root cause."

One of Doug's key talents is his ability to be rational and keep a calm head in the thick of a storm. When a problem arises or when he is deliberating on a decision that needs to be made, Doug automatically runs the scenarios through his mind: *What are the potential disasters? How can I effectively deal with these scenarios so I can avoid any traps? How can I work through the situation with minimal damage?* This intellectual skill is a trait that helps him avoid major problems, especially with being in the medical business, where his decisions could have a major impact on patients and their loved ones. Doug is thankful his companies have avoided any devastating issues.

A Leader Who Develops Other Leaders: Chris Wright

When you meet Chris Wright and hear his British accent, you can't help but smile. He is such a sincere and engaging person with a drive for success. Chris is from the small town of Filey, England, and he has always had a love for sports. He found his way to Minnesota and ended up working for the Minnesota Timberwolves' original owners, Harvey Ratner and Marv Wolfenson.

When businessman Glen Taylor bought the Timberwolves basketball team in 1994, he saw great talent in Chris, so he was the only executive retained. Chris worked for the new ownership group for one year under his old contract. When his one-year contract expired, Chris called Glen and asked, "What do you want me to do?"

Glen immediately replied that he would come to the office and meet with him.

When they met, Chris said he wanted to work under another contract, since he had always worked under one in the past. But Glen did not want to put Chris on a contract after seeing how well he treated his staff and clients, led people through problems, and built great relationships. Instead, he offered the following: "I want you to lead our business operation and run things for us. I won't let you down as long as you don't let me down. Don't worry about a contract; I'll never let your family down." The two shook hands.

Glen launched Chris into an exciting role because Glen saw the talent, trust, and unique qualities that Chris brought to the Timberwolves organization. It was a great fit for them both. Chris always told Glen that if he sold the team and left, he would also leave. So when Glen walked in one day after making up his mind not to sell, he said to Chris, "If we don't sell the team for another three or four years, will you stay?"

The answer was easy: "Yes!" Such decisions are much easier when you are following your passion, know your talents and use them on a daily basis, and work with people you trust and respect. But Chris didn't simply develop his own talents. As a leader, he knew that success depended on nourishing the talents of all his employees. In his words, "My key stakeholders are my . . . staff. So I try to put them at the center of everything I do on a day-to-day basis because the better I can make them, so goes our franchise." He says he is most proud of how he was able to develop and provide a culture where people could grow and excel.

The Timberwolves were no exception. Some grew so much they launched their own new careers. Examples include the former president of the Sacramento Kings, Chris

Granger; and the CEO of the Minnesota Timberwolves and Lynx (WNBA), Ethan Casson.

How could this culture be so effective? Chris, in part, credits the "One program," an onboarding process committed to one team, one community, and one voice that the Wolves developed for their new employees. They took onboarding seriously. Every new employee had lunch with Chris and the senior management team. Each person was assigned a mentor for one year to help him or her get launched and understand the Timberwolves and Lynx brand and culture.

As part of the "One program," they also did a follow-up with human resources after thirty, sixty, and ninety days plus a meeting with Chris after six months and one year. This was to ensure that the organization was doing what it said it would do and understood the team members' own aspirations. Chris asked each employee four questions:

- What was it like when we onboarded you?
- What were the first two weeks like?
- What were the next five months like?
- What do you aspire to in the next six months?

The systematic culture that enables talent to flourish is successful. Chris doesn't hire people just for their skill sets; they also need to fit into the culture. He wants each employee to be a brand ambassador for the team. To this day, Chris's approach is to find out what the customers' needs are and help them accomplish their goals. The employees he hires build relationships with their consumers, learn what they really need and want, and then align the consumers' feedback with how they can help. All of this allows employees to become brand ambassadors.

The trust between Glen and Chris remains to this day, even though Chris moved on when given the opportunity to pursue a dream of his: to start a local professional soccer team. In September 2017, he left the Timberwolves and Lynx. It's been twenty-four years since Chris and Glen shook hands, and Chris is now the CEO of the Minnesota United soccer team. All because someone saw the great match between his talent and the job. Chris is a great example of someone having passion for the responsibilities given and knowing and growing his talents. He embodies Bentley's core leadership lessons!

Look Back at Your Paw Prints—and Run Forward with Joy!

I took Bentley out today for a walk through one of the most beautiful wooded trails in Eden Prairie, Minnesota, a place called Birch Island. There, you can park your car and walk paths that wind gently through the woods. It is like a slice of heaven—calm and beautiful—that makes you feel so free. Bentley runs with joy back and forth on the path, veering off in directions that we've come to know so well together.

His way of looking at the beauty of the woods is by sniffing here and there and running ahead with his head up and back legs galloping like a horse. Then he stops and looks back to see where I am. He gazes up to the sky as if to say, *Hey, Dad, this is the greatest—being with you and being able to just be me!* I find it profound that he can show his enthusiasm, love, and excitement in such a natural way. It uplifts me. When he runs back to me just to say hello, I can't help but smile and thank God for this gift, Bentley. Here he is, overflowing with joy:

You can now run with joy too.

I want you to imagine for a moment that you are on a beautiful path with a canopy of large trees, which sets the stage as you walk through the woods, taking in the beauty of the lush green overhang and hearing birds singing their songs. You have graciously invited me and Bentley to join you for a short walk in this Birch Island sanctuary.

You ask me, "Robb, I have had real success thus far in my career, but I know I have much more to do and become. Where might I gain insight?"

I say, "Our calling and purpose are a natural extension of our talents and pure passion. Go back to chapter 1 and invest time to discover who you truly are. There is gold in your many God-given gifts, so let's figure out what they are! The exercises are a start, but you may want to go further and do a full battery of leader assessments—including emotional intelligence—so you can discover more inborn talents to use at work and in life."

We walk farther down the path, and you say, "You talked about Bentley getting out of the lake and shaking himself off until the water is gone. That seems to be an easy concept, but I have experienced heartache with people in my past. Is this important to deal with, or is it just a normal part of life? Does this hurt my ability to run with joy when I hold on to the hurt they've caused?"

I say, "Yes, it does. First, it is perfectly normal to know a few people whom you don't want to be around and to experience some angst when you see them or hear their names. You simply need to understand that extending forgiveness doesn't mean you have to be friends with them. Forgiveness is first for you so that you are free from encumbrances and can fully enjoy walking through life without carrying bitterness or worry.

"You may want to share with these people that you forgive them—and leave it at that. However, the better way is to begin a conversation with them and be understanding of their situations. This costs you nothing financially, and it allows you to be free of unwanted negative emotions that can drag you down. Take a look again at chapter 4."

We reach the end of the path, and you say, "I've tried to help people who have worked for me in the past in various ways, but I can't say I am an inspiring 'guide dog.' Any advice?"

I reply, "It is great to hear your honesty. I can tell by your question that you want to make a difference and become an inspiring 'guide dog' for others. If you know your talents and focus on what is in chapter 2—about being who you are—you'll find that your genuine relationship with others lays the foundation to gain wisdom in how best to guide people.

"Our role as leaders is to find out what motivates others and then help them bring out their best talents so they can reach their goals. In learning how to be an inspiring guide dog, you, in turn, will be inspired. When you sow good seed, you'll reap the good harvest in due time. When you see someone struggling, asking great questions will help them discover the answers. And yes, you will be helping everyone run with joy when you do."

Activate Your Gifts and Talents

Bentley truly lights up my life in so many ways every day. When I come home, there he is with his tail wagging, doing his magically happy greeting. We have much to learn from animals like Bentley, and we can apply this natural wisdom to everyday life. Think back now and remind yourself of the simple concepts you can learn from Bentley so you, too, can run with joy.

I know that information without insight is stagnation. When you are honest with yourself and you embrace change by following Bentley's leadership lessons, you can discover the greatness that is in YOU. But it will require taking action. So start running with joy by filling in the following exercise.

I will begin making a new paw print by taking these actions:

1. _____

2. _____

3. _____

PAW PRINTS TO REMEMBER

The questions and thoughts below will help you tackle the challenge of this first question: What is one step I can take to further *my own paw print for life*?

* Where are my passions? Do I know my talents today? (This is the essence of finding your "sweet spot" and taking your talents to a new level. To launch

effectively for yourself and your team members, you start with knowing and being who you are. It is at this point that you can unleash your God-given talents, face down those areas of disappointment, "shake off" your problems, and become a guide dog for others.)

🐾 How will I take action to rediscover my talents, motivating values, and the strengths of my style? (The brief exercises in this book give you a start, like kindling to a fire that wants to burst forth.)

🐾 What talents from my mini-360 do I want to start using a lot more and get better at?

🐾 What coaching do I need at this point? What skill development? (Just pick one and begin!)

🐾 Is there any area I need to "shake off," the way Bentley does when he comes out of the water? (Taking action toward resolving any past issues will bring you peace and the freedom to become what you *can* become.)

🐾 Who do you know on your journey who needs more guidance? Do you have room in your heart for someone else? If so, email them about what you are learning, and see what may come about!

Go, Bentley! Go, YOU! And best wishes on your new path.

Notes

INTRODUCTION

1. Jim Harter, "4 Factors Driving Record-High Employee Engagement in U.S.," *Gallup*, February 4, 2020, https://www.gallup.com/workplace /284180/factors-driving-record-high-employee-engagement.aspx.

CHAPTER 1

1. Jack Kelly, "More than Half of U.S. Workers Are Unhappy in Their Jobs: Here's Why and What Needs to Be Done Now," *Forbes*, October 25, 2019, https://www.forbes.com/sites/jackkelly/2019/10/25/more-than-half -of-us-workers-are-unhappy-in-their-jobs-heres-why-and-what-needs-to -be-done-now/#12bcf5e62024.
2. Plato, *Apology*, trans. Benjamin Jowett, The Internet Classics Archive, accessed on October 23, 2020, http://classics.mit.edu/Plato/apology.html.
3. *Encyclopaedia Britannica Online*, s.v. "Eudaimonia," accessed on October 23, 2020, https://www.britannica.com/topic/eudaimonia.
4. Matthew 25:14-30.
5. Plato, *The Republic*, trans. B. Jowett, Project Gutenberg.
6. William Shakespeare, *The Tragedy of Hamlet, Prince of Denmark*, The Complete Works of William Shakespeare, Act 1, Scene 3, http://shakespeare.mit.edu/hamlet/full.html.
7. Robert Burns, "To a Louse," Burns Country, accessed on October 24, 2020, http://robertburns.org/works/97.shtml.

CHAPTER 2

1. Amelia Rayno, "Feeling at Home, Hageman Becomes Face of Gophers Football," *StarTribune*, August 26. 2013, https://www.startribune.

com/feeling-at-home-hageman-becomes-face-of-gophers-football
/220958241/?refresh=true.

2. Rayno, "Feeling at Home."

3. Chris Tomasson, "Legal Problems Behind Him, 'Humbled' Ra'Shede Hageman Hoping for Another NFL Shot," *TwinCities*, March 27, 2019, https://www.twincities.com/2019/03/27/legal-problems-behind-him -humbled-rashede-hageman-hoping-for-another-nfl-shot/.

4. Master Tesfatsion, "Three to Watch: Local Players Headed for the NFL," *StarTribune*, May 6, 2014, https://www.startribune.com/three-to-watch -local-players-headed-for-the-nfl/258050701/?refresh=true.

5. Proverbs 3:13-18, 21-25.

6. Matthew 5:14-15.

7. Paraphrased from Eduard Spranger, *Types of Men*, trans. Paul John William Pigors (Tübingen, Germany: Max Niemeyer Verlag, 1928).

CHAPTER 3

1. *Online Etymology Dictionary*, s.v. "coach," accessed on October 24, 2020, https://www.etymonline.com/word/coach.

CHAPTER 4

1. In 2017, I was diagnosed with three other deadly cancers. In my book *The Power of 3*, I share the methodology I used to make it through the tough chemotherapy treatments, which I believe can be of help to anyone going through adversity.

2. Jackie Cooperman, "New Studies Suggest Emotional Intelligence Boosts Productivity," *Worth*, August 13, 2019, https://www.worth.com/new -studies-suggest-emotional-intelligence-boosts-productivity/; Harvey Deutschendorf, "Why Emotionally Intelligent People are More Successful," *Fast Company*, June 22, 2015, https://www.fastcompany.com/3047455 /why-emotionally-intelligent-people-are-more-successful.

3. Daniel Goleman, "Teach Emotional Intelligence in Schools," May 19, 2013, Linkedin, https://www.linkedin.com/pulse/20130519223058- 117825785-teach-emotional-intelligence-in-schools.

4. Christine Pearson and Christine Porath, *The Cost of Bad Behavior: How Incivility Is Damaging Your Business and What to Do about It* (London: Portfolio, 2009), 57–60.

5. Daniel Goleman and Richard E. Boyatzis, "Emotional Intelligence Has 12 Elements. Which Do You Need to Work On?" *Harvard Business Review*, February 6, 2017, https://hbr.org/2017/02/emotional-intelligence-has-12 -elements-which-do-you-need-to-work-on.

6. This is the first of several interviews I conducted with CEOs whose stories I share throughout the book.

7. "Faith and Religion," International Forgiveness Institute, accessed on October 30, 2020, https://internationalforgiveness.com/faith-and-religion .htm.

8. Anthony C. Holter, Joseph Martin, and Robert D. Enright, "Restoring Justice Through Forgiveness: The Case of Children in Northern Ireland," in *Handbook of Restorative Justice: A Global Perspective*, eds. Dennis Sullivan and Larry Tifft (New York: Routledge, 2008).

9. "Forgiveness Research," International Forgiveness Institute, accessed on October 30, 2020, https://internationalforgiveness.com/research.htm?mi=2.

10. "Enright Forgiveness Process Model," International Forgiveness Institute, accessed on October 30, 2020, https://internationalforgiveness.com/data /uploaded/files/EnrightForgivenessProcessModel.pdf.

11. "Enright Forgiveness Process Model."

12. "Enright Forgiveness Process Model."

13. "Jay Coughlin's Story," May 19, 2011, video, 5:35, https://www.youtube .com/watch?v=ysiwF1Vmeoo.

14. Kendra Cherry, "5 Components of Emotional Intelligence," Verywell Mind, January 24, 2020, https://www.verywellmind.com/components-of -emotional-intelligence-2795438.

CHAPTER 5

1. Lynn Buzhardt, "Guide Dogs," VCA Hospitals, accessed on October 30, 2020, https://vcahospitals.com/know-your-pet/guide-dogs.

2. Jim Clifton, "Beware of Managers from Hell," *Gallup*, March 22, 2013, https://news.gallup.com/opinion/chairman/169283/beware-managers -hell.aspx; Jim Clifton, "Millions of Bad Managers Are Killing America's Growth," *Gallup*, June 19, 2013, https://news.gallup.com/opinion /chairman/169208/millions-bad-managers-killing-america-growth.aspx.

3. Jim Harter, "4 Factors Driving Record-High Employee Engagement in U.S.," *Gallup*, February 4, 2020, https://www.gallup.com/workplace /284180/factors-driving-record-high-employee-engagement.aspx.

4. The positive business culture Paul Harmel created attracted Shutterfly to eventually purchase the company. The new owner disbanded the ESOP portfolios for the workers.

5. Paul Harmel, interview by Robb Hiller, April 14, 2014.

6. Harter, "4 Factors."

Acknowledgments

To make any book successful, you need an understanding team who can keep the home going when you are running from airport to airport. Because of my wife, Pam, I can do what I love to do.

Equally important is someone who brings love and energy to the home no matter what. That someone is our loving British Lab, Bentley. He's always happy, with his tail wagging and a smile on his face. We are thankful to God for allowing us to have Bentley as part of the family.

About the Author

A BUSINESS GRADUATE of St. Olaf College, Robb spent years working for Xerox and a few other larger firms before becoming one of the investors who took over a failing high-tech company, which he sold eight years later. Then, in 1995, after a six-month hiatus doing all the fun things he could think of, Robb became the founder and CEO of the consulting company Performance Solutions MN.

Today, Robb is nationally known for his expertise in talent selection, executive coaching, team development, sales, and leadership building. He was recently awarded the Bill J. Bonnstetter Lifetime Achievement Award for his extensive work in evaluating talent, having assessed more than 24,000 people in the past twenty-five years. Robb still believes that success is all about having the right people in the right jobs and growing their talent. Yes, strategy is important—and part of his practice as a trusted advisor to executives and sales leaders—but the right talent and teamwork are most important.

Over these past years, Robb has helped many companies and people get "unstuck." It is his passion. His vision for what he does is to help people and organizations discover how they can identify and ignite the use of their inborn talents so that they may become what they are meant to be—and experience greater success. Robb and his wife, Pam, have three adult children and live in Minnesota.

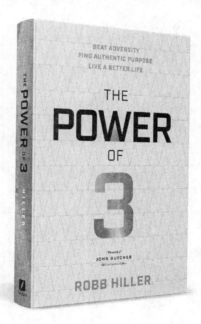

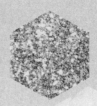